The Last Enemy to Be Destroyed

"Ralph Hawkins' *The Last Enemy to Be Destroyed* offers a hopeful Lenten journey through Scripture, exploring Christ's ultimate conquest of death itself. Hawkins poignantly reminds us that, 'because of Jesus's victory, we've got more future than we do past.' Enhanced by Sarah Hawkins' twenty evocative illustrations, this accessible work traces death's defeat from Genesis to Revelation. It provides a valuable resource for anyone seeking to understand this crucial aspect of the gospel and find freedom from the fear of mortality through Christ's victory."

—Bryan C. Hollon, dean and president, Trinity Anglican Seminary

"Lamenting Americans' tendency to deny death, Ralph Hawkins urges his readers to recognize its destructive power, while at the same time focusing on Jesus as the one who defeats death by death. *The Last Enemy to Be Destroyed* offers a richly informed Protestant account of the meaning of Christ's death as a substitutionary sacrifice. As an insightful guide steeped both in ancient Near Eastern cultures and in the Scriptures, Hawkins takes his readers on a hopeful Lenten journey to the final defeat of death."

—Hans Boersma, chair in ascetical theology, Nashotah House Theological Seminary

"It is a great gift when a scholar brings his or her knowledge to the work of a pastor, when a pastor exercises his or her ministry with the acumen of a scholar. In *The Last Enemy to Be Destroyed*, the Rev. Dr. Hawkins leads us thoughtfully and pastorally on a path that allows us to look squarely at our mortality—the worm at the core of our existence, the elephant in every room—and to grasp the victory over death that Jesus has won for us."

—David A. deSilva, trustees' distinguished professor of New Testament and Greek, Ashland Theological Seminary

"At a time when we take great pains to avoid facing the reality of death, Hawkins invites his readers to lay hold of the biblical witness concerning the place of death in the economy of salvation. Just as death entered by means of Adam's sin, so is it overcome by the victory of Christ on the cross who promises life everlasting to those he gathers into his mystical body. At once substantive and accessible, this devotional text is an ideal companion for the Lenten season."

—Alexander H. Pierce, assistant professor of historical theology,
North American Lutheran Seminary

"In stark contrast to the modern notion that death is the wholly natural end of our wholly material lives, Scripture makes clear that death is our enemy—indeed, our final enemy. In this lovely book, Ralph Hawkins comforts his readers through the biblical story of God's destruction of death 'by death,' culminating in death's final defeat by our Lord Jesus Christ."

—Joel Scandrett, associate professor of theology,
Trinity Anglican Seminary

The Last Enemy to Be Destroyed

The Problem of Death and the Ultimate Christian Hope

Ralph K. Hawkins

ILLUSTRATED BY
Sarah A. Hawkins

CASCADE *Books* • Eugene, Oregon

THE LAST ENEMY TO BE DESTROYED
The Problem of Death and the Ultimate Christian Hope

Cascade Books
An Imprint of Wipf and Stock Publishers
199 W. 8th Ave., Suite 3
Eugene, OR 97401

www.wipfandstock.com

PAPERBACK ISBN: 978-1-4982-9964-0
HARDCOVER ISBN: 978-1-4982-9966-4
EBOOK ISBN: 978-1-4982-9965-7

Cataloguing-in-Publication data:

Names: Hawkins, Ralph K., author. | Hawkins, Sarah A., illustrator.

Title: The last enemy to be destroyed : the problem of death and the ultimate christian hope / by Ralph K. Hawkins ; illustrated by Sarah A. Hawkins.

Description: Eugene, OR: Cascade Books, 2024 | Includes bibliographical references.

Identifiers: ISBN 978-1-4982-9964-0 (paperback) | ISBN 978-1-4982-9966-4 (hardcover) | ISBN 978-1-4982-9965-7 (ebook)

Subjects: LCSH: Death. | Death—Religious aspects—Christianity. | Hope—Religious aspects—Christianity.

Classification: BT825 H345 2024 (paperback) | BT825 (ebook)

VERSION NUMBER 11/08/24

In memory of
Rev. Greg Nunley
(1972–2017)

Contents

Acknowledgments

I would like to thank the staff of the Blount Library for their help with this project. Jessie Ross tirelessly secured references for me, and Dr. Jeremy Groskopf scanned Sarah's drawings in order to create digital versions. My appreciation goes to the congregations in which I have presented sermons on portions of this book, including Calvary United Methodist Church, Kerns Memorial United Methodist Church, and Grace Anglican Fellowship. As always, I am grateful to my wife, Cathy, and to our children, Hannah, Sarah, Mary, and Adam, for their love and support. Finally, I would like to thank Michael Thomson and Wipf & Stock for the opportunity to publish this volume with them. My prayer is that it may be a blessing to many. *Soli Deo gloria*!

Ralph K. Hawkins

Danville, Virginia
The Feast Day of Thomas à Kempis

Abbreviations

AB	Anchor Bible
ABD	*Anchor Bible Dictionary*. Edited by David Noel Freedman. 6 vols. New York: Doubleday, 1992
AEL	*Ancient Egyptian Literature*. Miriam Lichtheim. 3 vols. Berkeley: University of California, 1971–1980
BTCP	Biblical Theology for Christian Proclamation
CCC	Crossway Classic Commentaries
ConC	Concordia Commentary
COS	*The Context of Scripture*. Edited by William H. Hallo. 3 vols. Leiden: Brill, 1997–2002
CPNIVC	The College Press NIV Commentary
DBT	Discovering Biblical Texts
EBC	*The Expositor's Bible Commentary*. Rev ed. Edited by Tremper Longman III and David E. Garland. Grand Rapids: Zondervan, 2008

EI	*Encyclopedia of Islam.* Edited by Richard C. Martin. 2 vols. Farmington Hills, MI: Gale Cengage Learning, 2016
GSC	Geneva Series of Commentaries
HBD	*HarperCollins Bible Dictionary.* Edited by Mark Allan Powell et al. 3rd ed. San Francisco: HarperOne, 2011
NDBT	*New Dictionary of Biblical Theology.* Edited by T. Desmond Alexander and Brian S. Rosner. Downers Grove, IL: InterVarsity, 2000
NEASB	*Near East Archaeological Society Bulletin*
NICNT	New International Commentary on the New Testament
NICOT	New International Commentary on the Old Testament
NIB	*The New Interpreter's Bible.* Edited by Leander E. Keck. 12 vols. Nashville: Abingdon, 1994–2004
NIDB	*New Interpreter's Dictionary of the Bible.* Edited by Katherine Doob Sakenfeld. 5 vols. Nashville: Abingdon, 2006–2009
NIDOTTE	*New International Dictionary of Old Testament Theology and Exegesis.* Edited by Willem A. VanGemeren. 5 vols. Grand Rapids: Zondervan, 1997
TOTC	Tyndale Old Testament Commentaries
TWOT	*Theological Wordbook of the Old Testament.* Edited by R. Laird Harris et al. 2 vols. Chicago: Moody, 1980
TynBul	*Tyndale Bulletin*
WBC	Word Biblical Commentary

A Note about Style

ALL TRANSLATIONS FOLLOW THE New Revised Standard Version Updated Edition (NRSVue), unless otherwise indicated in the text. All transliterations follow the general-purpose style presented in the *SBL Handbook of Style*. Finally, in this volume, I follow the NRSVue's convention of rendering the divine name as "the LORD."

Preface

THIS SHORT VOLUME IS dedicated to the memory of my good friend, Rev. Greg Nunley, who succumbed to lymphoma on March 7, 2017. Although I had met Greg in passing sometime in 2013 or thereabouts, we did not get to know each other until after our daughters had become friends through the local theater in 2016. Our wives had begun coordinating a "game day" for our children, and during these times, Greg and I began enjoying what we came to call our "porch time." During these times, we would sit on the porch, sip coffee, and talk about Scripture, theology, and the preaching life. We had a lot in common, and we became close friends very quickly.

Greg continued serving as a pastor even while his cancer continued to worsen and his treatments weakened him. Since we were both preparing sermons every week during this time, during our "porch time" we would often talk about the lectionary passages, interpretive problems, which direction we were thinking about taking in our Sunday sermon, and which illustrations we were thinking about using. Sometimes, he would share about his illness and his feelings about his death, which seemed more and more immanent. During these conversations, we talked about the problem of death, the biblical claim that Christ has triumphed over death, and the question of when that triumph will be realized. I had run across two passages that really intrigued me, one in which Paul says that death will be "the last enemy to be destroyed" (1 Cor 15:26), and the other in which the author of Hebrews wrote that it was "by his death" that Jesus "broke the power of death" (Heb 2:14). We discussed these passages at great length, and the idea for a Lenten series based on them began to percolate in my mind. I began working on it, and preached the first installment on Ash Wednesday, March 1, 2017.

By the beginning of March, the doctors had said that Greg had only two or three days left. On Saturday, March 4, Greg asked me if I would bring him Holy Communion the next day. I brought it Sunday afternoon, but before we could celebrate it, Greg fell asleep. After he had slept about an hour, Stacy woke him up and we gathered around his chair with a few of the children. I shared a few words about John Wesley's sermon, "The Real Transubstantiation," in which Wesley explains that, during communion, it is not the bread and the wine that are transformed into the body and blood of Christ, but the worshipers themselves. I told Greg how grateful I was that our shared faith had brought us together and made us one in the body of Christ. We sang "One Bread, One Body," then I read the words of institution and gave everyone the elements. After I had given everyone else the elements, I asked Greg if he would serve me, and he did. As a concluding blessing, we sang "Shalom to You." It was a struggle for Greg to stay awake through it all, and moments after we finished, he was asleep again. Greg died the next night, around 11:30 p.m.

Greg was an inspiration to me because he never gave up hope, and even as his condition worsened, he never wavered in his faith. On Saturday, February 4, he sent me a text in which he said, "It seems I have found a very formidable adversary," and asked me to continue praying on his behalf. He continued preaching as long as he could and, in fact, preached on Sunday, February 26, just ten days before he died.

This volume grew out of the series of Lenten sermons that I first wrote in 2017 but have revised several times since then.

PREFACE

Although I initially conceived it as a Lenten devotional, its useful-
ness is certainly not limited to the Lenten season. I've also added
discussion questions at the end of each chapter, so that it may be
useful for Sunday School classes or book discussion groups. My
hope is that *The Last Enemy to Be Destroyed* will honor Greg's
memory, and my prayer is that it may encourage others who have
either lost a loved one or received a frightening diagnosis themselves. There will indeed come a day when the last enemy, death,
will be defeated, and our bodies will be redeemed.

Chapter 1

Ash Wednesday

The Fall and the Beginnings
of Death (Gen 3)

LENT IS A FORTY-DAY period of repentance and prayer in preparation for the celebration of Easter.[1] It begins with Ash Wednesday,
which is a day of penitence. In the Ash Wednesday service, there
is a congregational confession, and then worshipers go forward
and the pastor smudges ashes onto their foreheads in the shape
of the cross, with the words "Remember that you are dust, and to
dust you shall return." These words are a reminder of Gen 3:19,
which states that humans are dust.

The Ash Wednesday service is meant to remind us of our
mortality. As we head into the forty days leading up to Easter,
it's meant to remind us that, without the resurrection of Christ,
we have no hope in the world. Death prowls around everywhere,
threatening to destroy everything. It overcomes us all. It's "the last
enemy" of man and God (1 Cor 15:26).

In this volume, we are going to embark on a study entitled
"The Last Enemy to Be Destroyed," in which we're going to look at

---

1. Chittister, *Liturgical Year*, 108–13.

1

this imposing enemy and his eventual defeat. We're going to begin in this chapter by talking about the fall and the beginnings of death.

Original Blessing

If we're going to talk about the fall, we need to begin by talking about conditions before the fall. The story of creation is told in Gen 1, which has a highly poetic design.[2] Numerous words and phrases are repeated throughout, and this suggests that the author intended to present creation as the ultimate act of order. At every step of the way, God looked at what he had made and saw that it was "good" (*tov*). Everything God created was just as it was intended to be.[3]

When God created humankind, he put them in a garden, in Eden (Gen 2:8), where he blessed them with fertility and charged them with dominion (Gen 1:28). These were gifts given to humankind so that they could continue God's original designs for his creation.

Humankind was also blessed with God's close presence. The text doesn't explicitly say this, but Gen 2 repeatedly alludes to God's close presence with anthropomorphic language. God is the one who "formed man" (Gen 2:7); he "planted a garden" (2:8); and he "put" man in the garden (2:15). The point is that, in the garden, humans were near to God.

Humankind was created in a condition of what we could call "original blessing."[4] They were created in the image of God, lived in a pristine paradise, and enjoyed an unfettered relationship with God.

---

2. The question of the historical nature of Gen 1–2 goes far beyond our purposes here and cannot be examined in any detail. Opinions range from "it happened as it says" to "it's pure fiction." For a brief overview of the spectrum of opinion, see Goldingay, *Introduction to Old Testament*, 68–71.

3. Cf. Robert P. Gordon, "טוב (*ṭwb*)," *NIDOTTE* 2:35–57.

4. In contrast to the condition of original sin, which is a result of the fall. The idea of "original blessing" has been explored in Fox, *Original Blessing*; Shroyer, *Original Blessing*.

The Fall and the Beginning of Death

In Gen 3, the first couple, Adam and Eve, disobeyed the command of God, and the blessings began to unravel in a process that has come to be known as the "fall."[5]

Adam and Eve considering the forbidden fruit

In the fall, the man and woman experienced the judgment of blessing turned to curse, and its effects were extensive. Not only were Adam and Eve driven out of the garden, but the fall also brought biological, noetic, relational, and even ecological consequences.[6]

But was death a result of the fall? Eve told the serpent that God had said that she and Adam "shall not eat of the fruit of the

5. Again, whatever we make of the narrative, Gen 3 shows sin to be a violation of God's commandment. Guthrie explains, "The account of the Fall of Adam and its consequences puts in succinct form the common experience of mankind" (*New Testament Theology*, 118).

6. Cf. Allison, *Historical Theology*, 342–62.

tree that is in the middle of the garden, nor shall you touch it, or you shall die" (Gen 3:3). The serpent insisted that this wasn't true, and said, "You will not die" (v. 4). And it is true that, although Adam and Eve were driven out of the garden, Adam went on to live for a long time. In fact, he has the fourth longest lifespan in the Bible. According to Gen 5:5, he lived for 930 years. For this reason, some say that the warning that they would die when they ate the forbidden fruit "cannot be taken seriously."[7]

However, the author of Gen 3 makes it clear that the verdict of death *did* come about through the fall. And he does this by drawing a contrast between Adam's condition before and after the fall.[8] Whereas before the fall man was taken from the ground and given the "breath of life" (2:7), as a result of the fall he must return to the ground and the dust from which he was taken (3:19). This reversal emphasizes that "the verdict of death, warned of before the fall (2:17), had come about."[9]

We should understand that, even though Adam went on to live for many years, spiritual death was the immediate outcome of his disobedience. Spiritual death ensued immediately. The apostle Paul explains that, when the Ephesians were "following the course of this world, following the ruler of the power of the air," they were "dead through [their] trespasses and sins" (Eph 2:1). So separation and isolation from God leads to immediate spiritual death, and physical death is its by-product.

In Adam, All Die

In later Judaism, Jews believed that Adam's sin brought death into the world and placed all human beings under the power of sin and death. This is based on a group orientation, in which "individuals basically depend on others for their sense of identity, for their understanding of and their role and status in society, for clues to the

7. Barr, *Garden of Eden*, 10.

8. Just as he drew a contrast between the condition of the "land" before and after the fall in v. 18.

9. Sailhamer, "Genesis," 1:93.

duties and rights they have, and for indications of what is honorable and shameful behavior."[10] This sort of "corporate personality" was common in the ancient biblical world.

Modern Western readers may chafe at this way of thinking,[11] but the reality is that the fate of groups, even families and nations, are bound up together, regardless of whether they adhere to an ideology of collectivism or individualism. For example:

- In an economic context, the unethical behavior of a few could lead to a recession that affects an entire nation.

- In a military example, the failure of one soldier to observe proper military protocol could lead to the endangerment of an entire platoon or even an entire army.

- In an example related to harnessing thermal power through a nuclear power plant, the failure of a single employee to follow proper safety protocols could lead to the contamination or even the deaths of the inhabitants of the entire population living within its radius.

There is no escaping the fact that the one affects the many. And, based on this group orientation, Jews believed that Adam's sin brought death into the world and placed all human beings under the power of sin and death. This is a recurring idea in the texts of later Judaism.

The author of the Wisdom of Solomon, a book written by an Alexandrian Jew sometime between 100 BC and AD 50, explains that "God created us for incorruption and made us in the image of his own eternity, but through an adversary's envy death entered the world, and those who belong to his company experience it" (Wis

---

10. Neyrey, "Group Orientation," 88.

11. Western readers reject this idea because of the belief that persons are each and singly an end in themselves, and as such ought to realize their "self" and cultivate their own judgment, notwithstanding the push of pervasive social pressures in the direction of conformity. This individualist view, however, is really a recent Western innovation that can be attributed to the emphasis of the Puritans on the individual soul as being at the center of religion and the marketplace in sixteenth-century northern Europe.

2:23). Humankind was created in the image of God, but through Adam's sin, death entered the world.

Another important text for considering this issue is 4 Ezra, a late first-century AD Jewish apocalypse that explores the theological significance of the destruction of Jerusalem and its temple in AD 70. The author explains that the reason for Israel's sinfulness, which has led to the destruction of the temple, is the sin they inherited from Adam. He explains, "You laid upon him one commandment of yours, but he transgressed it, and immediately you appointed death for him and for his descendants" (2 Esd 3:7).

A bit later, he goes on to explain the consequences of Adam's sin in human history. He explains, "The first Adam, burdened with an evil heart, transgressed and was overcome, as were also all who were descended from him. Thus the disease became permanent; the law was in the hearts of the people along with the evil root, but what was good departed, and the evil remained" (2 Esd 3:21–22).

Later in the book, he complains that it would have been better if Adam had never been created, or if God had at least restrained him from sinning. But now, as a result of Adam's sin, the human condition involves sin and death (2 Esd 7:116–17). As he reflects on the impact of Adam's sin, he cries out: "O Adam, what have you done? For though it was you who sinned, the fall was not yours alone but ours also who are your descendants. For what good is it to us, if an immortal time has been promised to us, but we have done deeds that bring death?" (2 Esd 7:118–19).

These writings provide the background for Paul's own understanding. Paul explains to the Romans that "sin came into the world through one man, and death came through sin" (Rom 5:12), and that "many died through the one man's trespass" (v. 15), which "led to condemnation for all" (v. 18).

To the Corinthian congregation, he explains that "death came through a human," and that "all die in Adam" (1 Cor 15:21–22). Adam's sin introduced sin and death into the world. Through Adam, death was transmitted to the entire human race.

Death, the Last Enemy to Be Destroyed

Since the time of Adam, death has been prowling around everywhere, threatening to devastate everything. Jesus came and announced the kingdom of God (e.g., Mark 1:15), and indeed we experience many of its benefits even now.[12] Our sins are forgiven, we receive the Holy Spirit, and we've been raised up with Christ and seated with him in heavenly places (Eph 2:6).

And yet, the author of Hebrews says, "As it is, we do not yet see everything in subjection to them" (Heb 2:8–9). There's still evil in the world. We still struggle with sin. Paul says that even "we ourselves, who have the firstfruits of the Spirit, groan inwardly as we wait eagerly for our adoption to sonship, the redemption of our bodies" (Rom 8:23). But, until that final adoption takes place, Paul says, our bodies remain subject to death (8:10). Death is "the last enemy" of man and God (1 Cor 15:26).

Conclusion: Jesus Defeated Death . . . by His Own Death

The great mystery of the gospel is that Jesus came "so that *through death* he might destroy the one who has the power of death, that is, the devil, and free those who all their lives were held in slavery by the fear of death" (Heb 2:14–15; emphasis added). In these Lenten studies, we're going to explore *how* Jesus destroyed the last enemy—death—through his own death (1 Cor 15:26). And what we'll be able to see is that, because of Jesus's victory, we've got more future than we do past. "When we worship a victorious and risen Savior, we've always got more future than we do past."[13]

---

12. Cf. Kik, *Eschatology of Victory*.
13. Willimon, "Small Church Ministry."

Discussion Questions

1. What is the "fall," and what are its effects?

2. Read Gen 3:3. How can we reconcile the promise that death would be the result of Adam and Eve's disobedience with the fact that Adam went on to live for a total of 930 years?

3. How could the sin of one man place all humankind under the power of sin and death?

4. If Jesus launched the kingdom of God, then why are humans still subject to death?

Chapter 2

Death as an Enemy

WE LIVE IN A death-denying culture.[1] There are many factors that contribute to and perpetuate the denial of death, including: the avoidance of the topic, the use of euphemisms to refer to it, the relegation of the care of the dying and the deceased to professionals, and the façade the funerary industry puts over the reality of death.[2] More and more frequently, the traditional funeral is replaced with a "celebration of life." In a traditional funeral, the body of the deceased is present, and a funeral service follows a liturgy that acknowledges the power of death and the fact that a death has occurred. In contrast, in a celebration of life, the body of the deceased is absent, and the emphasis is on remembering the life of the loved one and honoring his or her achievements.[3] In recent years, I have attended celebrations of life in which not only was the body of the deceased absent, but the fact that they had died was never mentioned and those leading the service insisted that it was an occasion for merriment.

1. Cf. Becker, *Denial of Death*.

2. For a brief discussion of each of these and others, see Hawkins, *Ancient Wisdom*, 200–201.

3. Long, *Accompany Them with Singing*, 6–7.

In this chapter, we will explore the meaning and implications of death. If Adam's sin brought death into the world, what exactly does that mean? What is death? Is it natural? Or is death something to be feared? Is the death of our loved ones cause for celebration or mourning? How should we, as Christians, view death?

What Is Death?

There are a number of terms that define the Old Testament concept of death. The most common Hebrew word is the noun *mawet*, which simply means "death" (e.g., Ps 6:6). In Canaanite religion, there was a god of death called Mot, and sometimes Old Testament texts personify death by using this name for it (e.g., Jer 9:20).[4]

But what is death? And what happens to people when they die? The basic definition of death, according to Wikipedia, is "the irreversible cessation of all biological functions that sustain a living organism."[5] But does this mean that people cease to exist when they die? In both the Old and New Testaments, the dead don't appear to cease to exist, but they go to the "abode of the dead." There are several terms for the abode of the dead in both Testaments.

Sheol

In the Old Testament, the most common term for the abode of the dead is *sheol*. This term for the underworld occurs sixty-six times in the Old Testament. There is very little description of it, but there are some occasional glimpses. Some passages seem to describe it as a vast, subdivided burial chamber (e.g., Ezek 32:21–28). It is not entirely clear in the Old Testament who goes to Sheol. Some argue that only the wicked went to Sheol, but it appears that people in the Old Testament world saw it as the place where all the dead went.[6]

---

4. There are additional terms for death too (Richards, "Death," 2:108).
5. "Death," para. 1.
6. E.g., Barr, *Garden of Eden*, 29–30.

Those who go to Sheol are sometimes called "shades" (*rephaiym*), which are "lifeless, nebulous, shadowy creatures in the underworld," who "never have any contact with the living."[7] It also seems that they are alienated from God. In Ps 88, the psalmist complains that he is "like the slain who lie in the grave, whom you remember no more, who are cut off from your care" (v. 5 NIV). He goes on to ask the LORD about the state of the dead:

> Do you show your wonders to the dead?
>> Do their spirits rise up and praise you?
> Is your love declared in the grave,
>> your faithfulness in Destruction?
> Are your wonders known in the place of darkness,
>> or your righteous deeds in the land of oblivion?
> (vv. 10–12 NIV)

It seems that these shades can't praise the LORD (Ps 88:10), and they're so lethargic that they have to be roused whenever somebody new arrives in Sheol (Isa 14:9–10). Sheol seems to be a lifeless place, where its inhabitants are half asleep (e.g., Isa 14:9–10).[8]

7. Cf. Moyer, "Shades."

8. Sleep is a common metaphor for death in the Old Testament (e.g., Ps 90).

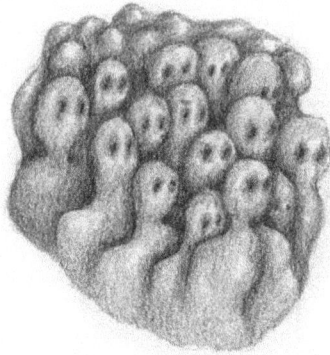

Shades in Sheol

Hades

In the third century BC, when Greek-speaking Jews translated the Old Testament into Greek, they rendered the Hebrew word Sheol with the Greek word *Hades*, which was the realm of the dead in Greek mythology. It seems that the Jews conceived of Sheol in much the same way the Greeks thought of Hades, as a general abode of the dead. In both cases, it was seen as a shadowy underworld, where existence was miserable and not life in any full sense.

The Quality of Life in the Abode of the Dead

However, in both Sheol and Hades, it was thought that there was a sort of continuance. People were not extinguished at death. And they could even recognize each other in the realm of the dead.

- In *The Odyssey*, Odysseus knows his mother in Hades. Her face and shape are the same as they have been during life. However, there is no bodily substance, and when he goes to embrace her, his hands pass right through her.[9]

- In the Old Testament, after he has died, Samuel appears to Saul as a shade and is recognized by his cloak and his general manner (1 Sam 28:11–14).

Saul prostrate before the ghost of Samuel

- In the New Testament, Jesus tells the parable of the rich man and Lazarus, in which the rich man recognizes Lazarus from Hades (Luke 16:19–31).[10]

9. Homer, *Odyssey*, bk. 11.

10. It appears that the rich man is suffering in Hades, while Lazarus is "with Abraham" (Luke 16:22–23). The separation of Hades into a place for punishment and torment for the wicked and a place of happiness for the righteous appears to have developed in the intertestamental period. Even after this

In both the Old and New Testaments, death was not viewed as a total extinction. There was a sort of existence after death, but it was a shadowy existence that could scarcely be called life.

How Was Death Viewed in Biblical Times?

In light of all this, how was death viewed in biblical times? Was it viewed positively or negatively?

As the Natural End of Life

In one sense, death was seen as the natural end of life. And there are passages all through the Old Testament that record what we could call the "good" deaths of the Old Testament saints. The report about the death of Abraham, for example, reads this way: "This is the length of Abraham's life, one hundred seventy-five years. Abraham breathed his last and died in a good old age, old and full of years, and was gathered to his people" (Gen 25:7–8).

---

development, however, Hades is still viewed as the abode of all the dead, as a holding place until the resurrection, when Hades will give up all its dead (Rev 20:13).

The death of Abraham

In this view, a "good" death is when someone dies with plenty of children and at an old age.[11] From this perspective, it's just natural that humankind is mortal[12] while the LORD is immortal,[13] and death was viewed as a problem only when it came prematurely.

With Fear, Anger, and Hostility

The predominant view of death in the Old Testament, however, is negative. There are many Old Testament passages about the fear of death. One of the most poignant is the description of death at the end of the book of Ecclesiastes:

11. E.g., Gen 25:8, 46:30.
12. E.g., 2 Sam 14:14.
13. E.g., Ps 18:47.

Remember your creator in the days of your youth, before the days of trouble come and the years draw near when you will say, "I have no pleasure in them"; [2] before the sun and the light and the moon and the stars are darkened and the clouds return with the rain; [3] in the day when the guards of the house tremble, and the strong men are bent, and the women who grind cease working because they are few, and those who look through the windows see dimly; [4] when the doors on the street are shut, and the sound of the grinding is low, and one rises up at the sound of a bird, and all the daughters of song are brought low; [5] when one is afraid of heights, and terrors are in the road; the almond tree blossoms, the grasshopper drags itself along, and the caper bud falls; because all must go to their eternal home, and the mourners will go about the streets; [6] before the silver cord is snapped, and the golden bowl is broken, and the pitcher is broken at the fountain, and the wheel broken at the cistern, [7] and the dust returns to the earth as it was, and the breath returns to God who gave it. [8] Vanity of vanities, says the Teacher; all is vanity. (Eccl 12:1–8)

Here, the reader is confronted with the fact that "among all the images of the undoing of nature no death is more profound than the reader's own," and "there is certainly a deep sense of fear in being brought before this reality."[14]

It seems that fear, though, is not the main reaction to death in the Old Testament. We more often find reactions of anger and hostility in the face of death. We find these kinds of sentiments expressed most often in the Psalms and some of the wisdom literature. In Ps 6, for example, the psalmist cries out:

> O Lord, do not rebuke me in your anger,
>   or discipline me in your wrath.
> Be gracious to me, O Lord, for I am languishing;
>   O Lord, heal me, for my bones are shaking with terror.
> My soul also is struck with terror,
>   while you, O Lord—how long?
> Turn, O Lord, save my life;

14. Richards, "Death," 2:109.

deliver me for the sake of your steadfast love.
For in death there is no remembrance of you;
    in Sheol who can give you praise?
I am weary with my moaning;
    every night I flood my bed with tears;
    I drench my couch with my weeping.
My eyes waste away because of grief;
    they grow weak because of all my foes. (Ps 6:1–7)

In Ps 90, the psalmist laments the transience of life and the seeming permanence of death. He exclaims:

You turn us back to dust,
    and say, "Turn back, you mortals."
For a thousand years in your sight
    are like yesterday when it is past,
    or like a watch in the night.

You sweep them away; they are like a dream,
    like grass that is renewed in the morning:
in the morning it flourishes and is renewed,
    in the evening it fades and withers. (Ps 90:3–6)

Another powerful example is in Ps 102, which reads, in part:

Hear my prayer, O LORD;
    let my cry come to you.
Do not hide your face from me
    in the day of my distress.
Incline your ear to me;
    answer me speedily in the day when I call.
For my days pass away like smoke,
    and my bones burn like a furnace.
My heart is stricken and withered like grass;
    I am too wasted to eat my bread.
Because of my loud groaning
    my bones cling to my skin.
I am like a desert owl of the wilderness,
    like a little owl of the waste places.
I lie awake;
    I am like a lonely bird on the housetop.
All day long my enemies taunt me;

those who deride me use my name for a curse.
Indeed, I eat ashes like bread
and mingle tears with my drink,
because of your indignation and anger,
for you have lifted me up and thrown me aside.
My days are like a lengthening shadow;
I wither away like grass. (Ps 102:1–11)

Each of these passages reflects the anger, frustration, and anxiety of its author over death.

Jesus's Reaction to Death

Even Jesus reacted to death—or to the threat of death—with deep emotion.

A Man with Leprosy (Mark 1:41)

On his first preaching trip through the Galilee, a man afflicted with leprosy came to Jesus and begged him to make him clean (Mark 1:40). In biblical times, the word "leprosy" was used to designate a wide variety of skin diseases. It wasn't limited to what we know today as leprosy or, to use the medical term, Hansen's disease. In biblical times, "leprosy" was a general term.

But whatever variety of skin disorder the man had, it caused him a lot of suffering. And this suffering would have been social as well as physical. The law required that "the person who has the defiling disease shall wear torn clothes and let the hair of his head be disheveled, and he shall cover his upper lip and cry out, 'Unclean! Unclean.' He shall remain unclean as long as he has the disease; he is unclean. He shall live alone; his dwelling shall be outside the camp" (Lev 13:45–46). This was probably because it was not fully understood. People were afraid of it and associated it with death.

Instead of keeping his distance as the law demanded, this leper came right up to Jesus and fell down on his knees to make his plea. He apparently didn't have any doubt that Jesus could heal him; he wondered only whether Jesus was willing.

What I want to focus on here, though, is Jesus's reaction to the man, in v. 41, which is very unusual. The NRSVue says that Jesus was "moved with pity," which led him to reach out, touch the leper, and heal him. But the NIV says that Jesus was "indignant," which means angry.

That seems so strange. "Jesus was angry," and so he reached out and touched the man and healed him. Why would Jesus be angry? There have been all kinds of theories about why Jesus might have been angry. One suggestion is that Jesus was angry because the man approached him, whereas according to the Mosaic law he should have avoided all human contact; however, Mark goes on to say that Jesus voluntarily touched the man, making himself ritually unclean, and this hardly indicates displeasure with the man's action. Another proposal is that Jesus might have been angry with the leper's doubts about Jesus's willingness to heal him. When the leper approached Jesus, he did say, "If you are willing" (Mark 1:40). Another explanation attributes the anger to the fact that Jesus has been interrupted in his preaching tour, but this is totally in conflict with Mark's presentation of Jesus's mission as one in which preaching and healing go hand in hand.

The best answer is probably that Jesus's anger wasn't directed at the leper at all, but that he was angered by the presence of a death-dealing disease that could only be the work of the devil.[15] Jesus's anger wasn't focused on the man or on the disease, but on Satan whose machinations were destroying the lives of precious people. If we understand the incident in this way, it becomes an example of the fierce conflict between Christ and Satan that plays such an important part in his ministry.

The Death of Lazarus (John 11)

The story of the raising of Lazarus provides a moving example of Jesus's reaction to the death of one of his close friends. The text notes that Jesus was close friends with Mary, Martha, and their

---

15. Wessel and Strauss, "Gospel of Mark," 9:721.

brother Lazarus, who lived in Bethany. It says he "loved" them (v. 5). Lazarus became deathly ill, and so they sent word to Jesus, saying, "Lord, he whom you love is ill" (v. 3).

Lazarus died before Jesus arrived in Bethany (v. 14) and, when he got there, he found Mary weeping, and there were many Jews with her who were also weeping. And the text says that, when Jesus saw this, "he was greatly disturbed in spirit and deeply moved" (v. 33). He asked them to take him to the grave, and when they arrived, he himself began weeping (v. 35).

Jesus wept.

Then the text notes again that Jesus was "again greatly disturbed" (v. 38 NRSV). Jesus's response here as "greatly disturbed" (*brimaomai*) and "deeply moved" (*tarrasso*) is so important. Gail O'Day cogently observes that, while Jesus's reaction could be interpreted as one of deep compassion, the Greek verbs used here actually communicate agitation and indignation.[16]

She stresses that it is important not to sentimentalize Jesus' reaction and his tears, and that these verses highlight the bitter cost and power of death in human lives and so underscore the significance of Jesus' ultimate victory over death.[17]

Conclusion: Acknowledging the Power and Finality of Death

So far in this series, we've been talking about the power of death. It is one of the main characters in the biblical story. "Death stalks around everywhere, threatening to destroy everything."[18] In the biblical world, death was a visible fact of life to everyone. When death came to someone in the family, the family had to manage it themselves.

Pastor Fleming Rutledge points out that it wasn't until "about a hundred years ago [that] we started calling in the morticians to hustle the bodies out of sight." She goes on to explain that it is "Not so in these tender-minded times. Our culture is infamous for its unceasing attempts to manage death, to get it out of sight, to perfume it and embalm it and cover it with flowers."[19]

She even criticizes memorial services, because "they celebrate the person's life independently of the power of Death."[20]

Rutledge insists that "there can be no true proclamation of the Resurrection until there has been an acknowledgment of the power and the finality of Death. It is indeed 'the obscene mystery, the ultimate affront, the thing that cannot be controlled.'"[21]

16. O'Day, "Gospel According to John," 9:690.
17. O'Day, "Gospel According to John," 9:690–91.
18. Rutledge, *Undoing of Death*, 272.
19. Rutledge, *Undoing of Death*, 274.
20. Rutledge, *Undoing of Death*, 276.
21. Rutledge, *Undoing of Death*, 276.

But when we come face-to-face with the power of death, then we can really come to appreciate Jesus's victory over it. And that's the wonderful message of the gospel, that Jesus came "so that *through death* he might destroy the one who has the power of death, that is, the devil, and free those who all their lives were held in slavery by the fear of death" (Heb 2:14–15; emphasis added).

By his power, thank God, we can be free from the power of sin and death (Rom 8:2).

Discussion Questions

1. What is death?

2. What do the terms Sheol and Hades mean, and how do they relate to one another? What did ancient peoples believe was the quality of life for those who went to Sheol or to Hades?

3. How was death viewed in biblical times? Was it viewed as a cause for celebration?

4. How did Jesus react to death?

5. What is really required in order to fully appreciate Jesus's victory over death?

Chapter 3

How Can the Enemy Be Overcome?

IN CONTEMPORARY AMERICAN SOCIETY, we pretend that death is not real. Our aversion to death has led to the development of an entire industry designed to put a façade over the reality of death. Tony Evans caricatures the ways the funerary industry does this.[1] He notes that funeral parlors have professional makeup artists who dress up the deceased and make them look as lifelike as possible, and exclaims that "I've seen some people look better dead than they ever looked alive." He observes that, at the visitation, the head of the deceased is carefully positioned on a satin pillow, as if they were resting comfortably. And he satirically notes how the casket is eased into the ground by a nickel-plated machine, so as not to wake the deceased. The American way of death is all about denying it.[2]

As we saw in the last chapter, however, death is a devastating consequence of sin, which is viewed in the Bible as a great enemy. But if death is the great enemy, then how can it be overcome?

1. Evans, *Book of Illustrations*, 72.

2. Becker, *Denial of Death*; Mitford, *American Way of Death*; Mitford, *American Way of Death Revisited*.

Throughout history and across cultures, the answer has been the same. Sin and death are very serious and cannot be escaped through denial. They are viewed so seriously, in fact, that they can be overcome only by the death of an innocent victim, sacrificed on behalf of others.

The Human Universal of Sacrificial Atonement

In cultural anthropology, which is the study of human culture, there is a concept called the "human universal."[3] A *human universal* is a belief or practice that has been common to humanity across time and culture throughout human history. Some examples of human universals include:

- The use of clothing—throughout human history, people have felt a sense of shame about their nakedness and have designed clothing to cover it
- The organization of people into kinship units
- The development of language

These are just some examples, but you get the idea. There are some things that people everywhere, throughout human history, have believed and done.

And throughout human history and across cultures, people have had an innate sense that sin and death can be overcome only by the sacrificial death of an innocent victim offered on their behalf. And when we look back across the history of human culture, we see that sacrificial systems appear in virtually every religious system. David Levinson notes that sacrifices were conducted for a wide variety of reasons, including "to remove sin, assuage guilt, win favors, avoid punishment, bond with gods and spirits, give gods or spirits what is theirs, maintain the order of the universe, avoid conflict, resolve disputes, and celebrate events of personal, family, or community or religious significance."[4]

3. Brown, *Human Universals.*
4. Levinson, "Sacrifice and Offerings," 379.

But at their core, sacrifices were understood to address the relationship between people and the supernatural world. Levinson explains that "the animals sacrificed . . . are meant to please a supernatural force . . . and to maintain or reestablish the bonds between the believers and their supernatural world."[5] The theological term for this is *sacrificial atonement*, in which the word "atonement" refers to the status of being at one with the deity.

Among the primal religions, sacrifice has played a very prominent role. The Nuer, a group concentrated in the Nile region of Africa, in the South Sudan, are a prime example. In Nuer religion, there is a category of sin that includes serious breaches, like adultery or incest, that are regarded as "death." Sins in this category are so serious that they will lead to death, and the only way the threat of death can be avoided is through sacrifice. And these sacrifices require the death of an ox, the most precious possession any Nuer could possibly own. When he sacrifices an ox to god, a Nuer man is said to be enacting, through the victim, his own personal death. Once the atonement is complete, the god can finally "turn away," and the family, clan, or tribe can be relieved that it is out of danger.[6]

5. Levinson, "Sacrifice and Offerings," 379.
6. Evans-Pritchard, *Nuer Religion*.

Animal sacrifice in Nuer culture

When we turn to the world's major religions, we see the same phenomena. In Hinduism, for example, sacrifice has traditionally played a very important role. In the earliest centuries, sacrifice was very personal. But as Hinduism became more complex and institutionalized, during the Vedic period, sacrifice took on a central role and came to be seen as vital for maintaining the cosmic order by appeasing the gods. Indian society produced a great deal of literature on sacrifice, and priests became the experts in conducting it.

China's oldest religious practice consisted of sacrifice to Shang Di, the high god of heaven. There was a special sacrifice known as "the Great Sacrifice," which was performed every year at the Temple of Heaven by the emperor himself in order to atone for the sins of the people. The Great Sacrifice was very elaborate and included: (1) the selection of the sacrificial animals three months in advance; (2) a proclamation by the emperor himself announcing the upcoming sacrifice; (3) the inspection of the sacrificial animals five days in advance of the sacrifice; (4) a fast by the emperor that began three days before the sacrifice; (5) a second inspection of the sacrificial animals three days before the sacrifice; (6) a third inspection of the animals two days before the sacrifice; (7) a procession to the Altar of Heaven complex on the day of the sacrifice; and (8) nine ceremonies carried out at the altar itself.[7] Chinese traditions claim that all eighteen dynasties worshiped Shang Di in this way, and that twenty-two emperors made 654 sacrifices to Shang Di at the Altar of Heaven.

Burnt offerings to Shang Di on the altar at
the Temple of Heaven

In ancient Israel, animal sacrifice was a practice that spanned the people's history. It had been practiced by Israel's earliest ancestors, Abraham, Isaac, and Jacob.

---

7. The History of the Han Dynasty (1100 BC) explains the ceremony and its importance. Incidentally, the Great Sacrifice has many parallels to the Day of Atonement ritual (Lev 16).

Sacrifice in the ancestral period

Later, with the rise of Mosaic religion, ritual sacrifice was the primary ritual activity. In the period after the exodus, when the Israelites wandered in the wilderness, they made their sacrifices at the tabernacle. The book of Leviticus gives detailed instructions for these sacrifices, which we'll look at more closely in chapter 5.

Sacrifices at the tabernacle altar

In Islam, all Muslims on the Hajj perform an animal sacrifice, while those who have stayed home, all over the world, participate in the sacrificial slaughter in their own communities in the ' *id al-Adha*, the Festival of Sacrifice.[8] The sacrifices are to commemorate Abraham's willingness to sacrifice his son Ishmael in obedience to Allah's command, Ishmael's obedient decision to be sacrificed, and Allah's provision of an animal sacrifice so that Ishmael's life was spared.[9] The sacrifices also represent the individual Muslims' desire to be obedient to Allah by making sacrifices in their own lives that will help them to remain on the "straight path" of Islam.

While the ritual is not for the purpose of atonement, some Muslims may believe their slate is wiped clean by the sacrifice.

Some Caribbean religions, like Santeria and Vodoun, still practice animal sacrifice today.[10] In Santeria, sacrifices are made

8. Azam, "Religious Holidays and Observances."

9. In the Old Testament, Abraham sacrifices Isaac, whereas in the Qu'ran, he sacrifices Ishmael.

10. Murrell, *Afro-Caribbean Religions.*

to secondary gods called "orishas" in order to nourish their life force. Blood offerings provide the orishas with the power to work for the benefit of human devotees. It is only when blood offerings are made that the orishas "can and usually do become responsive to the needs of the individual making the offering."[11] In Vodoun, goats, cows, sheep, pigs, chickens, doves, and dogs can be sacrificed, and sacrificial offerings are actually required to feed the spirits "for the maintenance of the protective relationships they have with their [devotees]."[12] There is also an annual ritual in Vodoun called the *peye san* (paying for blood), in which the blood of a sacrificial animal is dabbed on the forehead of an initiate or a community member for protective purposes.[13]

In all of these cases, there is a belief that the blood of a substitute provides safety, wholeness, well-being, or reconciliation with the spirits or a god.

A Deity Must Be the Sacrifice

It's long been recognized that many cultures also had the idea that the god must provide or even *be* the sacrifice.[14] There are many examples. In a famous tale of Phoenicia, the god Cronus begat an only son, called Jeud. And, when the nation was endangered by a war, he dressed his only son in the emblems of royalty and offered him up as a sacrifice on an altar as a divine-human substitute.[15]

There are many myths in which the great divine heroes give themselves up unto death in order to secure redemption. Examples include Osiris in Egypt, Dionysus in Greece, Attis and Adonis in western Asia. In these cases there was no sense of sin associated

---

11. De La Torree, *Santería*, 47.

12. Hebblethwaite and Weber, "Arabian Religion, Islam," 232.

13. Hebblethwaite and Weber, "Arabian Religion, Islam," 233.

14. E.g., Goodspeed, "Atonement in Non-Christian Religions." In this classic article, Goodspeed references many of the classic history of religions works that explore this idea.

15. Eusebius, *Preparation for the Gospel*, 1:10.29.

with the death of these gods, but simply an annual death and resurrection that ensured the continued well-being of the people.

In Old Norse mythology, there's a ninth-century poem called "Hávamál," in which the god Oden sacrifices himself to himself. He says, "Nine nights I hung upon the Tree, wounded with the spear as an offering to Oden, myself sacrificed to myself."[16] This strange passage seems to show the god giving himself up in order to accomplish the work of salvation.

Oden sacrificed on the world tree

Modern Myths of Substitutionary Atonement

The idea of substitutionary atonement is so deeply ingrained in the human psyche that it even appears repeatedly in our own modern-day myths—science fiction and superhero stories. Here are just a few examples.

16. "Hávamál" 138, in Lindow, *Handbook of Norse Mythology*, 164–65.

In *Star Trek 2: The Wrath of Khan*, the tyrant Khan has stolen the Genesis Device, a technology that can reorganize matter in order to create habitable worlds for colonization. When Khan is mortally wounded, he activates the Genesis Device, which will reorganize all matter in the nebula, including the *Enterprise*. Captain Kirk's crew detects the activation of Genesis, and they try to move out of range, but because the ship's warp drive was damaged in the battle, it becomes clear that they will not be able to escape the nebula in time. Spock goes down to the engine room to fix the warp drive, but McCoy tries to stop him, since exposure to the high levels of radiation would be fatal. But Spock incapacitates the doctor with a Vulcan nerve pinch.

Spock enters the engine room and successfully restores power to the warp drive, and the *Enterprise* is able to escape the explosion, but it costs Spock's life. Kirk bursts into the engine room and finds Spock dying of radiation poisoning, and the two share a few poignant moments together. As Spock lies dying in Kirk's arms, he tells him that he should not grieve, because his decision to sacrifice his own life to save those of the ship's crew was the logical one. He explains, "The needs of the many outweigh the needs of the few or the one."[17]

In *Harry Potter and the Deathly Hallows: Part 2*, Harry, the hero, is known as the "Chosen One." He is the only one who is believed to be able to defeat the villain, Voldemort. However, there is a piece of Voldemort's soul within him. In order to destroy this piece of Voldemort's soul, Harry himself would have to die. He goes to the Forbidden Forest to confront Voldemort, who casts the killing curse upon him. It appears that Harry dies, and he goes into limbo, where his former mentor Dumbledore's spirit meets him and explains to him that Voldemort's own curse has destroyed the fragment of his soul that resided within Harry. As a result, Harry is able to return to his body, resolved to finally and permanently defeat Voldemort.[18] There were many other times in Harry's life where he could have died but chose the safety

17. Meyer, *Star Trek II*, 1:30:58–39:30.
18. Yates, *Harry Potter*, 1:22:36–42:49.

of others over his own: his encounters with the basilisk, the De-
mentors, giant spiders, and the dangerous people he came across.
Harry could have chosen to save himself, but he put his life on the
line for the safety of everyone else around him.

Spider-Man 2 focuses on the conflict between Spider-Man
and Doctor Octopus. At one point, as they battle, they fall onto
a rapid transit train. Doctor Octopus sabotages the controls and
leaves the train hurtling toward disaster. Spider-Man positions
himself on the front of the train as it hurtles toward certain
doom, and tries to use his webbing to stop the train. He stops the
train at the last possible second and collapses from the strain. The
grateful passengers gingerly bring him back into the train car,
and as they pass him over their heads to safety, he sprawls out in
the shape of a cross.[19]

In the season finale of season 1 of *Supergirl*, Supergirl's enemies Non and Indigo decide to use a device called Myriad to kill
everyone on Earth and then to conquer the rest of the universe.
They increase Myriad's signal to a level that will cause everyone's
minds to blow, and only four hours remain to try to find the
signal's source. Once the device is found, it's discovered that no
human can get near the device without being killed. Supergirl is
the only one who can save the planet, and she is willing to give
herself up on humanity's behalf.

She goes around telling her friends and loved ones how
much she loves them, but without letting them know what she's
about to do. Finally, she flies the device into space, knowing that,
when she does so, she will no longer be able to fly nor breathe.
This means she will not be able to fly back to Earth and will die
in outer space. But Supergirl loves humankind so much that
she does it anyway, and once she pushes the device out beyond
the atmosphere, she drifts aimlessly into space and lapses into
unconsciousness. She's saved at the last moment when her sister
uses the pod that brought her to Earth to save her.[20]

---

19. Raimi, *Spider-Man 2*, 1:37:23–41:47.
20. Teng, "Better Angels."

Substitutionary Atonement in Religion and Myth

Why does this idea that people can ultimately be saved only by the sacrifice of an innocent victim appear throughout history and across cultures, in all known religions and myths? In a now-famous letter that C. S. Lewis wrote to his friend Arthur Greeves on October 18, 1931, Lewis explains that the reason the world's myths contain these ideas is that the ideas are true. Whereas the stories of the gods giving themselves up for humankind are myths, "the story of Christ is simply a true [story]: a [story] working on us in the same way as the others, but with this tremendous difference that it really happened."[21] And he goes on to explain, "One must be content to accept it in the same way, remembering that it is God's [story] where the others are men's [stories]: i.e., the pagan stories are God expressing Himself through the minds of poets, using such images as He found there, while Christianity is God expressing Himself through what we call 'real things.'"[22]

This theme of substitutionary atonement appears throughout the religions, myths, and stories of humanity because God has placed eternity in the hearts of men (Eccl 3:11). God made humankind to know within their hearts that they cannot atone for their own sin, but that such atonement must come from outside themselves.

It must come from an innocent one, given on their behalf. Modern people are likely to chafe against this concept. Why in the world would one life have to be given up in order to save the life of another? The idea sounds horrible and offends modern sensibilities. The principle, however, may be illustrated by the use of a vaccine in the prevention of the spread of a disease. In order to prevent the spread of the disease, people are injected with a vaccine, which is a dead version of the disease.

---

21. Lewis, *Family Letters*, 977.

22. Lewis, *Family Letters*, 977. For more on myths and fairy tales as expressions of timeless truths and pervasive human longings, see Lewis, *God in the Dock*, 63–67; Buechner, *Telling the Truth*, 73–98.

Sacrifice is the same way. A victim is offered up for a penitent. And, as we have seen, most cultures throughout history have offered up animals as sacrifices. But some recognized that this was not enough, and they wrote stories in which the gods offered up an only begotten child, or even themselves, as the sacrifice.

Conclusion: Christianity as a True Story

The author of Ecclesiastes knew long ago that God has placed eternity in the hearts of all people (Eccl 3:11). This means that humankind had an innate sense of the divine, and of their separation from the divine due to their own sin. Even more, throughout human history, men and women have known within their hearts that they cannot atone for their own sin, but that such atonement must come from outside themselves. This innate sense has found expression in the stories, myths, and religions of the world—even the modern ones. And these truths find their fullest expression in the true story of the gospel, which teaches that Jesus came "so that *through death* he might destroy the one who has the power of death, that is, the devil, and free those who all their lives were held in slavery by the fear of death" (Heb 2:14–15; emphasis added). Thanks be to God, "just as Christ was raised from the dead by the glory of the Father, so we too might walk in newness of life" (Rom 6:4).

Discussion Questions

1. What are "human universals"?

2. What is substitutionary atonement? Is the perceived need for substitutionary atonement a human universal?

3. In world mythology, who must ultimately provide the sacrifice?

4. How does the idea of substitutionary atonement feature in modern myths?

5. Why does the idea of substitutionary atonement appear throughout history and across cultures, in all known religions and myths?

Chapter 4

The Passover Sacrifice

THERE WAS A MAN who was out with his wife when they got caught in a terrible hailstorm. It was a frightening storm, with hailstones as big as baseballs. The man realized that he could not get his wife to safety in time and that, if he did not act quickly, she could be severely injured or even killed. He acted fast and draped himself over her, so that the stones pummeled him instead of her. The baseball-sized stones hurtled from the sky and pummeled the man so that his ears and head were bleeding. Although he tried to move them toward cover, he finally collapsed, sprawled over his wife as a protective cover. They both survived, but the man bore scars that were perpetual reminders of that day when he provided a protective cover for her so that the storm passed over her without harming her.[1]

In the foregoing chapters, we have been looking at the imposing enemy of death and its eventual defeat. So far, we've talked about the fall and the beginnings of death; about how death is an enemy; and about how the world's religions and mythologies all recognize that the only way sin and death can be overcome is through substitutionary atonement, when an innocent victim is

1. This true story is recounted in Evans, *Book of Illustrations*, 257–58.

37

sacrificed in place of the one making the offering. In this chapter, we will look at how this idea is manifested in the Old Testament's foundational salvation event—the Passover. When the angel of death passed through ancient Egypt and slew the firstborn child in each house, the angel *passed over* the houses of those who had marked their doorways with the blood of a spotless lamb. That first Passover was memorialized in an annual meal celebrating the protection of those who trusted in the LORD for their salvation.

God Calls Moses and Sends Him Back to Egypt

It all begins in the book of Exodus, which opens with the Hebrews enslaved in Egypt. Moses, who had grown up in Egypt, had fled into the wilderness after having killed an Egyptian taskmaster in defense of a Hebrew. He had lived among the Midianites for forty years in a sort of self-imposed exile. Then, the text recounts that "after a long time the king of Egypt died. The Israelites groaned under their slavery and cried out. Their cry for help rose up to God from their slavery. God heard their groaning, and God remembered his covenant with Abraham, Isaac, and Jacob. God looked upon the Israelites, and God took notice of them" (Exod 2:23–25).

God called Moses to go confront Pharaoh and demand their release (Exod 3:7–10). Accompanied by his brother, Aaron, Moses confronted Pharaoh and demonstrated the power of God by turning a staff into a snake (7:8–13). But Pharaoh was unimpressed, and his heart "became hard and he would not listen to them" (7:13).

The Ten Plagues

The LORD then sent a series of ten plagues upon Egypt, in order to try to impress upon Pharaoh that he was the LORD (7:17). These plagues were a series of disasters and climatological catastrophes. The plagues have often been interpreted as the result of natural phenomena, a cause-and-effect chain. There may have been some cause-and-effect at work in the ecological disasters of the plagues. However, even if the author of Exodus ever considered this possibility, he was not interested in the plagues as natural phenomena, but viewed their cause in divine terms.

In fact, the biblical author understood the plagues as having been directed by the LORD against particular Egyptian deities.[2] The plagues were God's judgment against Egypt, by which the LORD would make "fools" (*'ālal*) of the Egyptians (Exod 10:2). God himself said that, in the plagues, he would execute judgments against all the gods of Egypt (12:12).

This view of the plagues is born out in later biblical traditions. In the book of Numbers, Moses says, "The LORD executed judgments even against their gods" (Num 33:4). And the intertestamental literature follows this view. The author of the Wisdom of Solomon explains that the Egyptians were punished by their own idolatry. He argues that the very creatures they thought to be gods were the very cause of their punishment: "For when in their suffering they became incensed at those creatures that they had thought to be gods, being punished by means of them, they saw and recognized as the true God the one whom they had before refused to know. Therefore the utmost condemnation came upon them" (Wis 12:27).

The pseudepigraphic book of Jubilees (48:5) also teaches this:

> And the LORD executed a great vengeance on them for Israel's sake, and smote them through blood and frogs, lice and dog-flies, and malignant boils breaking forth in blains; and their cattle by death; and by hail-stones, thereby He destroyed everything that grew for them; and by locusts which devoured the residue which had been left by the hail; and by darkness; and by the first-born of men and animals, and on all their idols the LORD took vengeance and burned them with fire.[3]

2. Currid, *Ancient Egypt*, 104–20; Hawkins, *Discovering Exodus*, 94–103; Sarna, *Exploring Exodus*, 63–80.

3. Charles, *Book of Jubilees*, 205.

The first plague, in which the Nile was turned to blood, had a powerful theological meaning. The waters of the Nile, which were so critical to the Egyptians, were deified. The ancient Pyramid Texts call the Nile River by the divine name Hapi.[4] The "Hymn to the Nile" taught that life in Egypt came from the Nile.[5] When the Nile was turned to blood, it would have killed the fish, which were a staple of the Egyptian diet. The theological meaning of this plague was that, because of the disaster from the hand of the LORD, Hapi could no longer take care of the Egyptian people.

In the second plague, the plague of frogs, the amphibians fled from the uninhabitable Nile. The Egyptians thought of the frog as a symbol of divine power and a representation of fertility. One of the main goddesses of Egypt was Heqt, who was pictured as a human female with frog's head. She was the wife of the creator god, Khnum. When Khnum made humans on his potter's wheel, she assisted as midwife at their births and blew the breath of life into them. She also controlled the multiplication of frogs in Egypt by protecting the frog-eating crocodiles. But the LORD overwhelmed her, showing that it was he who really controlled fertility, and the frogs became a curse upon Egypt.

The third and fourth plagues both involved flying insects, gnats and flies. The third plague involved *kinnim*, a Hebrew word whose meaning is unclear, though it likely refers to gnats, or maybe to vermin, lice, or maggots. The fourth plague involved either a stinging fly or possibly a mosquito. These plagues may have been aimed at Kheprer, the god of resurrection, who was symbolized by the flying beetle.

The fifth plague involved pestilence on the domesticated animals of Egypt (Exod 9:1–7). Livestock animals provided many necessities, including food, milk, clothing, and transportation. These animals were extremely important. Because of their value in Egyptian society, bull cults flourished throughout the land in antiquity. They were viewed as fertility figures, and Apis was the most important of such sacred bulls. There were also a number

---

4. Mercer, *Pyramid Texts*, 4:65.

5. Lichtheim, "Hymn to the Nile."

of important goddesses portrayed as livestock animals, including Isis and Hathor.

The sixth plague, the infestation of boils, was probably a polemic against Sekhmet, the lion-headed deity of plagues. She was responsible for epidemics in ancient Egypt and was supposed to have the power to heal those who were visited by pestilence.

The seventh plague, which involved hail, was probably a mockery of sky deities, including Nut, female representative of the sky and personification of the vault of heaven. There were other sky deities, like Shu, who held up the sky, and Tefnut, the goddess of moisture. The plague of hail demonstrated that none of these deities could control the sky, but that it was the LORD who really had authority over it.

Locusts were a perennial problem in ancient Egypt, and the deity Senehem was supposed to be able to protect the country against ravages by these pests. A ton of locusts, which is a tiny part of the average swarm, eats the same amount of food in a single day as 10 elephants, 25 camels, or 2,500 people. A locust swarm could leave a country barren within days. The eighth plague, a locust infestation, revealed Senehem's powerlessness to protect the Egyptians from this destructive force.

The ninth plague was an attack on Amon-Re, the chief deity of Egypt, who was the personification of the sun. The rising of the sun in the morning symbolized new life and resurrection, and its setting symbolized death and the underworld. Because of the way his symbolism reflected the creation and destruction of life, the Egyptians considered him the creator god, and the "Hymn to Amon-Re" calls for universal reverence to him.[6]

The tenth and final plague is described as a "disease" (*nega*) (11:1) that would strike down every firstborn son in Egypt (11:5). This was the culmination of all the plagues and, in certain respects, the most severe. It has to be understood in terms of the concept and status of the firstborn in ancient times.[7] The firstborn had a

6. Ritner, "Great Cairo Hymn."

7. Cf. Exod 13:2, 12, 13, 15; 22:28–29; 34:19; Lev 27:26; Num 3:13, 40–46; 18:15; Deut 15:19.

special status of sanctity and preciousness. In both law and society, the firstborn had preference in inheritance and the right of succession.[8] In Egypt, Pharaoh's firstborn had preeminence in society. He was the crown prince and would inherit the throne. Since Pharaoh was viewed as a god in Egypt, the transference of the throne to his son in dynastic succession was the way that the god maintained his rule over Egypt without interruption.

In the eyes of the LORD, of course, Pharaoh was not a god, and no divinity would be transferred to his son when he inherited the throne. Conversely, the LORD was the true God of all humankind, and since Israel was his "firstborn son," it was the Pharaoh who should, in fact, treat Israel with deference. Moses said as much when he first returned to Egypt and spoke to the Pharaoh, saying: "Thus says the LORD: 'Israel is my firstborn son. I said to you, "Let my son go that he may serve me. But you refused to let him go; now I will kill your firstborn son"'"(Exod 4:22–23). The tenth plague, therefore, was primarily directed against the Pharaoh as a god of Egypt and against Pharaonic succession.

And the plague on the firstborn was directly administered by the LORD himself. The LORD explained to Moses that "I will go throughout Egypt," and "every firstborn son in Egypt will die, from the firstborn son of Pharaoh, who sits on the throne, to the firstborn son of the female slave, who is at her hand mill, and all the firstborn of the cattle as well. There will be loud wailing throughout Egypt—worse than there has ever been or ever will be again" (11:4–6 NIV).

The text repeatedly states that it was the LORD himself who would smite the firstborn in Egypt. He reiterated, "On that same night *I* will pass through Egypt and strike down every firstborn of both people and animals, and *I* will bring judgment on all the gods of Egypt. *I* am the LORD" (v. 12 NIV; emphasis added). The Israelites were commanded to stay indoors because *the LORD* would go throughout the land to strike down the Egyptians (12:23). And, "at midnight, [it was] *the LORD* [who] struck down all the firstborn in the land of Egypt, from the firstborn of Pharaoh who sat on the

---

8. Gen 43:33, Deut 21:17.

throne to the firstborn of the prisoner who was in the dungeon and the firstborn of all the livestock. Pharaoh arose in the night, he and all his officials and all the Egyptians, and there was a loud cry in Egypt, for there was not a house without someone dead" (12:29–30; emphasis added). Clearly, the author wanted to emphasize that it was *the* LORD who struck down the firstborn of Egypt!

Strangely, 12:23 states that it was the "destroyer" (*mishkhith*) who actually entered the houses and struck down the firstborn. There have been a variety of interpretations of this destroyer. Some have interpreted it as some kind of primitive demon.[9] Others have seen it as a sort of "death angel" acting in the LORD's service.[10] Still others have understood it as an extension of the LORD himself. William Propp identifies it as "a personalized, quasi-independent aspect of Yahweh."[11] However the destroyer is to be understood, it is clear that it was under the LORD's control and was considered his emissary.[12] It was the LORD himself who struck down the firstborn of Egypt. This plague of death would demonstrate the absolute sovereign power of the God of whom the Pharaoh had denied all knowledge.

The Passover

How were the Hebrews to be saved from this plague of death? The LORD explained to Moses that, in preparation for the night of the final plague, each man was to take a lamb for his family. The lamb should be a year old and without defect. At twilight, they were to slaughter the lamb, take some of its blood, and put it on the sides and tops of the doorframes of the houses (Exod 12:1–6).

9. Gray, *Sacrifice in Old Testament*, 364–65.

10. 2 Sam 24:15–17, 2 Kgs 19:32–37.

11. Propp, *Exodus 1–18*, 409.

12. Durham, *Exodus*, 163.

The slaying of the Passover lamb

Painting the post and lintel with the blood of a spotless lamb

They were to prepare the lamb and eat it as a meal inside the home. They were to eat it dressed and ready to go—with "your loins girded, your sandals on your feet, and your staff in your hand, and you shall eat it hurriedly" (12:11).

Eating the first Passover meal

That night, the LORD would come through Egypt and strike down the firstborn, thereby bringing judgment on all the gods of Egypt (Exod 12:12). "The blood," however, "will be a sign for you on the houses where you are, and when I see the blood, I will pass over you" (v. 13 NIV). In Israel, blood was viewed as constituting the life essence. In Lev 17:11, the LORD explains, "The life of the flesh is in the blood, and I have given it to you for making atonement for your lives on the altar, for, as life, it is the blood that makes atonement."[13] A life had to be poured out in substitution in order to provide atonement.

The Passover lamb was understood as a sacrifice (Exod 12:27). And when the LORD saw the blood of the lamb painted onto the doorways of the Israelite houses, the English translations say that he "passed over" them. The word translated as "pass over" is the Hebrew *pesakh*, and there is a lot of debate about where this word comes from.[14] It probably comes from the unattested Hebrew verb *pasakh*, which would mean "to protect." If that's the case, then *pesakh* means "protection." In this case, v. 13 would read "when I

---

13. Cf. Gen 9:4, Lev 17:14, Deut 12:23, Ps 72:14.
14. Hendrik L. Bosman, "פֶּסַח," *NIDOTTE* 3:642–44.

see the blood, I will protect you."[15] When the LORD saw the blood of the spotless lamb, he would protect the Israelites from death.

Whether we translate it as "pass over" or "protect," the implications are the same. The blood of the spotless lamb caused the LORD to "pass over" the Israelites, thus protecting them from death. And that's exactly what happened. That night, the angel of death passed through Egypt, and all the firstborn of Egypt were slain (Exod 12:29–30). This was an attack on Egypt's religion and their very identity. In the death of Pharaoh's firstborn, the Egyptian cycle of dynastic succession was interrupted, which demonstrated the LORD's total superiority over the Pharaoh and the Egyptian gods. With this final plague, the Pharaoh finally agreed to let the Hebrews go (vv. 31–32). Pharaoh, his officials, and all the Egyptians urged the Israelites to leave the land of Egypt, and Israel also plundered the Egyptians by taking their jewelry and clothing (12:31–36). The Israelites left after having lived in Egypt for 430 years.

The Passover Festival

The fact that the Passover triggered the exodus was paramount. It led to the Israelites' freedom, to their becoming a nation. After the first Passover, instructions were given for a Passover festival to be celebrated annually in Hebrew homes. During this festival, a ritual meal would be eaten while the events of the first Passover were rehearsed. The Passover ritual was fashioned into a catechism, a question-and-answer format in which children ask their parents about the events of the first Passover so that the story can be retold around the table (12:24–27). While it came to be known as the "Passover Festival" (Exod 34:25), it could just as well be translated as the "Protection Festival," because it commemorates how the blood of the spotless lamb protected the Israelites from the plague of death and led to their liberation from slavery in Egypt. For American readers, a close analogy could be the Fourth of July, which commemorates American independence. The

---

15. This is given as an alternate reading in the JPS translation (Tigay, "Exodus," 118).

Passover Festival celebrates early Hebrew independence as a nation but, more importantly, spiritually.

Conclusion: Passover and Progressive Revelation

The happenings of that first Passover were foundational events in the Old Testament. They charted the spiritual direction of early Israel in a process of "progressive revelation."[16] The original Passover demonstrated the idea that Israel would always be dependent on the LORD for its salvation, which would be based on substitutionary atonement. And the Passover ordinance, which was to be celebrated every year in the Passover Festival, reinforced this idea.

This was the case until God finally raised up a Messiah in Israel, who for three years preached that, through him, God would finally bring full and complete salvation to Israel. He said that this would happen when he suffered and died on Israel's behalf.[17] On the evening of his arrest, Jesus shared a Last Supper with his disciples (Mark 14:22–25), in which they were actually celebrating the annual Passover Festival.

During the meal, Jesus profoundly reinterpreted several of its elements. When he took the Passover bread and broke it, he said, "This is my body" (Mark 14:22). In the past, it had reminded the Israelites of their quick departure from Egypt. From now on, Jesus said, it should remind them of his body, which was about to be broken on the cross for them. Then Jesus took the cup, which recalled the blood of the Passover lamb, poured out for the Israelites for their protection, and he held it up and said, "This is my blood of the covenant, which is poured out for many" (Mark 14:24). In Israelite history, the annual celebration of the Passover had always been a reminder of what the LORD had done for the

---

16. Cf. the classic explanation in Hodge, *Systematic Theology*, 1:446; Orr, *Problem of Old Testament*. For contemporary articulations of the doctrine, see Graeme Goldsworthy, "Relationship of Old Testament and New Testament," *NDBT* 81–89; Packer, "Understanding the Bible."

17. The three passion predictions in the Gospel of Mark are a classic example of such teaching (Mark 8:31, 9:30–31, 10:33–34).

Israelites when they were slaves in Egypt.[18] But now, Jesus said, "Do this in remembrance of *me*" (Luke 22:19; emphasis added). And so that "Last Supper" became the *new Passover* meal, which Christians call Holy Communion. It celebrates Jesus's saving work as the fulfillment of the Passover.

Jesus celebrating the Last Supper with his disciples

The next day, as Jesus hung on the cross, the Jews asked Pilate to have the legs of the crucified be broken so the Sabbath laws wouldn't be violated by having their bodies hanging on the crosses after sundown (John 19:31). The Roman soldier thought Jesus might already be dead, so he pierced his side instead (vv. 32–34). And John explains that this happened so that the Passover regulations

18. Exod. 12:2–3; Num 9:1–2; Deut 6:20–23, 16:1.

would be followed, that none of the bones of the Passover lamb would be broken (v. 36; Exod 12:46). He understood Jesus's death on the cross through the lens of the Passover sacrifice. He understood Jesus as the *perfect* and *final* Passover sacrifice. Through the sacrificial death of Jesus on the cross, the Old Testament institution of the Passover was finally being fulfilled.

And you and I reap the benefits. Paul says, "For our Paschal Lamb, Christ, has been sacrificed" (1 Cor 5:7).[19] And, on the basis of that sacrifice, the Destroyer "passes over us," we're saved from the death plague, and we're united fully and finally with God through Jesus Christ.

Discussion Questions

1. What was the leading salvation event in the Old Testament?

2. How does the idea of substitutionary atonement feature in the story of the first Passover?

3. What was the meaning of the annual Passover festival?

4. What is "progressive revelation"?

5. How did Jesus reinterpret the Passover? What is the new Passover meal, and what is its significance?

---

19. The term "paschal" comes from *pesach*, the Hebrew word for Passover.

Chapter 5

The Old Testament Sacrificial System

MY OLDER BROTHER AND I were both born on the Marine base in Yuma, Arizona, in the 1960s, during the Vietnam war. My father served as an avionics technician, working on fighter jets that were deployed to Southeast Asia. There was a list of all the Marines on the base, and every so often, the ones at the top of the list would be deployed. Every time that happened, those whose names had been lower on the list would be moved toward the top. This worried my parents terribly because, by this time, they had two babies at home. My father's name got closer and closer to the top, but when it became evident that he could be deployed, someone without children volunteered to go in his place. And this happened more than once. When my parents told me this story many years later, I was deeply moved. If these other young men had not sacrificed themselves by going to Vietnam in my dad's place, my brother and I would probably have grown up without a father.

In chapter 3, we talked about how, all across the ancient world, there was a belief that death could be defeated only when an innocent victim was sacrificed on one's behalf. This belief manifested itself in sacrificial systems in all the world's major religions and in myths of gods giving up their one and only sons, or even themselves, on behalf of their people. In this chapter, we will return to the exodus period to look at the sacrificial system that was implemented among the early Israelites at Mt. Sinai.

The Revelation of the Sacrificial System

In the ancient Near East, sacrifice was well known as the way to appease the gods. Sacrifice was certainly not unique to ancient Israel, but was also widely used in other cultures. Animal, grain, and drink offerings to deities were common to the religious cults of Mesopotamia and Syria-Palestine. The widespread use of sacrifices throughout the ancient Near Eastern world attests to the universally recognized need to placate the gods.[1] In and of itself, sacrifice was not a special revelation to the Israelites.

The special revelation to Israel lay in the way that God made use of this feature of ancient Near Eastern culture as part of progressive revelation. This cultural knowledge became a "contextual vehicle" that God could use to teach the Israelites about the one, true God and how sin must be dealt with in relation to him.[2] It was distinctive from all the other sacrificial systems of the ancient Near East in that it was directed toward the goal of personal and communal holiness.[3]

The Sacrificial System

There were five basic types of sacrifices that were instituted as part of ancient Israel's system of worship in ancient Israel, all of which are presented in detail in the book of Leviticus.[4] These were the:

1. Brown, *Human Universals.*
2. See the discussion of "contextual vehicles and contextual givens" in Goldingay, *Introduction to Old Testament,* 133.
3. Walton, *Ancient Near Eastern Thought,* 131–32.
4. For detailed study, see Sklar, *Leviticus.*

1. Burnt offering (1:3–17)

2. Grain offering (2:1–16)

3. Peace offerings (3:1–17)

    a. Thank offering

    b. Vow offering

    c. Freewill offering

4. Sin offering (4:1—5:13)

5. Guilt offering (5:14—6:7)

These sacrifices can be roughly divided into two categories. The first consists of those offered to God in praise and thanksgiving for blessings received or favors granted. These include the grain offering and the three types of peace offerings. These offerings were thankful responses to the goodness of God.

The second category contains those required by the LORD on the occasion of sin in the Israelite community. These include the burnt offering, the sin offering, and the guilt offerings. These offerings were all required to purify the holy place from the desecration brought on by sin, and they led to reconciliation with God and restored the penitent sinner to fellowship with other people and God.[5]

There was also an annual ritual called the Day of Atonement, which made atonement for all Israel, including both the priesthood and the people (Lev 16).

How It Worked

The rationale for the sacrificial system is found in Lev 17:11, which says that "the life of a creature is in the blood, and I have given it to you to make atonement for yourselves on the altar" (NIV). The word "atonement" has to do with purifying people or

---

5. For one of the most comprehensive discussions of sin and how it was dealt with the sacrificial system, see Boda, *Severe Mercy*, 49–85.

things of sin[6] so that they are no longer under the wrath of God.[7] Through the sacrificial offering, the penitent person is rendered clean and can be reconciled with God.

The process involved five steps. First, a person would bring their gifts to the entrance of the tent of the presence before the LORD.[8] Second, in the case of blood offerings, those who brought the offering would lay their hand on the head of the animal and confess their sins.[9] The laying on of hands probably represented the transfer of sins to the animal, which served as a substitute for the sinner.[10] The third act was the slaughtering of the animal, which was usually done by those who had brought the animal.[11] The fourth act was the sprinkling of the blood, which would be done by the priests, who would sprinkle it on the horns of the altar. The leftovers would be poured out at the base of the altar,[12] while the other parts of the animal were given to the priests and burned either as a whole or in part, depending on the kind of offering being made.[13]

---

6. Cf. Green, "Atonement."

7. Cf. Richard E. Averbeck, "כפר," *NIDOTTE* 2:708.

8. Lev 1:3; 3:1, 12; 4:4.

9. Cf. Lev 5:5, 16:21.

10. Cf. Gen 22:13, Deut 3:26, Isa 53:12.

11. Cf. Lev 1:4, 11; 3:2, 8, 13; 4:14, 24. Sometimes, the priest (Lev 1:15) or even the high priest (4:3) would slaughter the animal.

12. Lev 16:14–15; 4:5–7, 18, 25, 30, 34.

13. Cf. Lev 1:9, 13, 17; 3:9–11, 14–17; 4:8–10, 19, 26, 35; Exod 29:13.

Priests conducting sacrifices at the temple altar

Special rules applied on the annual Day of Atonement, since it provided atonement for the sins of the entire nation. In this case, a bull was sacrificed as a sin offering to make atonement for the priesthood (Lev 16:11–14). Then a goat was sacrificed to provide atonement for all Israel (vv. 15–17). And, finally, another goat was presented, and the high priest would lay his hands on its head and recite over it "all the wickedness and rebellion of the Israelites—all their sins—and put them on the goat's head" (v. 21a NIV). This goat would then be released into the wilderness to "carry on itself all their sins to a remote place" (v. 22 NIV). This "scapegoat" was not slaughtered but driven away, carrying the sins of Israel with it.

The Sacramental Nature of the Sacrificial System

The Old Testament makes it clear, though, that the sacrificial rituals did not work automatically. And it's not that they bought God's forgiveness either. Animal sacrifice was not some kind of quid pro quo that automatically saved people or earned them a ticket to heaven.

The sacrificial system has to be understood symbolically. Behind the symbolism stood a request for atonement and the presentation of that request in the carrying out of the ritual sacrifice. But only God could actually grant forgiveness or provide atonement.[14] Andrew Hill and John Walton explain:

> The believer under the old covenant was counted as righteous on the basis of faith in YHWH and faithfulness to the covenant and its stipulations (e.g., Gen. 15:6; Hab. 2:4). The external act of ritual sacrifice was symbolic and representative of the internal attitude and disposition of the heart. Psalmists, sages, and prophets reiterated the truth that God does not desire sacrifice, but repentance leading to obedience (cf. 1 Sam. 15:22–23; Ps. 51:16–17; Prov. 21:3; Isa. 1:12–17; Jer. 7:21–23; Hos. 6:6; Amos 5:21–24; Mic. 6:6–8).[15]

The reality was that God removed people's guilt and forgave their sins when they confessed those sins and prayed to God for forgiveness.[16] God would grant forgiveness to anyone who truly repented. The sacrificial ritual was the place where the Israelites could present their requests for reconciliation, and their sacrifices in some sense symbolized those requests. When God favorably accepted their sacrifices, he also willingly forgave their sins so long as restitution was made whenever possible (Lev 6:4–6).[17]

Christoph Barth, son of the famous Swiss theologian Karl Barth, calls the message of the sacrificial system revealed at Sinai "the Sinai gospel."[18] Similarly, John Goldingay calls it "Israel's Gospel."[19] The reason is that the proper observance of sacrifice

---

14. Barth, *God with Us*, 164.

15. Hill and Walton, *Survey of Old Testament*, 88.

16. E.g., Exod 32:11–13, 30–35; Isa 6:5–7.

17. Israel's "sacramental awareness" is evident in the fact that, after the tabernacle and the temple cease to exist, the drama of the Day of Atonement continues (Brueggemann, *Reverberations of Faith*, 14).

18. Barth, *God with Us*, 165.

19. Goldingay, *Old Testament Theology*.

restores right relations with God and allows the resumption of life under blessing.

Conclusion: The Sacrificial System and Jesus the Messiah

The purpose of Hebrew sacrifice was to worship God and facilitate his presence in the midst of the Hebrew community. Ultimately, however, the sacrificial rituals "served to instruct the Israelites in the principles of God's holiness, human sinfulness, substitutionary death as a response to human transgression, and the need for repentance."[20]

Furthermore, the sacrificial rituals provide the interpretive lens for understanding the redemptive work of Jesus the Messiah. John the Baptist recognized and announced that Jesus was the Lamb of God who takes away the sins of the world (John 1:29–34). And Jesus himself understood his role as that of the Good Shepherd who lays down his life for his sheep (John 10:1–21).

The apostle Paul says that we have "been justified by his blood" and that, although we were enemies of God, "we were reconciled to God through the death of his Son" (Rom 5:9–10).

The author of Hebrews connects the death of Jesus with the Day of Atonement ceremony and interprets his death as the ultimate atoning sacrifice (Heb 9–10).

The apostle John, in his epistles, also identifies Jesus with the sacrificial victims of the Old Testament. He says, "He is the atoning sacrifice for our sins, and not only for ours but also for the sins of the whole world" (1 John 2:2 NIV), and "This is love: not that we loved God, but that he loved us and sent his Son as an atoning sacrifice for our sins" (1 John 4:10 NIV).

When we say, "Christ died for my sins" or we're "saved by the blood" of Jesus, it's because we believe that Jesus was the fulfillment of the Old Testament sacrificial system.

---

20. Hill and Walton, *Survey of Old Testament*, 89.

Discussion Questions

1. Was animal sacrifice in the ancient Near East unique to the Israelites?

2. How did the cultural knowledge of sacrifice become a "contextual vehicle" that God could use to teach the Israelites?

3. What were the five basic types of sacrifices in ancient Israel? What was the rationale for the sacrificial system?

4. What does it mean that "the sacrificial rituals did not work automatically"? And, if they did not work automatically, how did they work?

5. What was the ultimate purpose of the Old Testament's sacrificial rituals?

Chapter 6

Good Friday

The Sacrificial Servant
in the Prophets

IN THE PRECEDING CHAPTERS, we have seen that there is a great irony in Scripture: death is defeated by death. In the book of Exodus, God commands a Passover lamb to be sacrificed in order to rescue the Israelites from the angel of death and free them from slavery in Egypt. At Mt. Sinai, God institutes a sacrificial system that calls for the regular sacrifice of cattle in order to atone for sin. And, once we get into the prophets, we see that they begin to teach that, eventually, the LORD would send a man, a Servant, his Son, to die on behalf of humankind once and for all. In this chapter, we will look at several of these prophets and their prophecies of a Suffering Servant.

Isaiah's Suffering Servant

Isaiah was called to be a prophet in the eighth century BC, during a time of a crisis of national impurity, and many of his prophecies are pronouncements of judgment on the nation of Judah. In addition to his prophecies of judgment, though, Isaiah also prophesies about the future restoration of Judah, which he envisions would be brought about by a messianic figure.[1] This messianic theme is so prominent, in fact, that Isaiah is sometimes referred to as the messianic prophet.[2] One of the most celebrated passages in the book is Isa 52:13—53:12, which is the fourth in a series of passages known as the Servant Songs that describe an anonymous figure called the "Servant of the LORD."[3] This Servant of the LORD is described as someone who suffers horribly and yet emerges victorious.

The passage starts out by giving a sort of overview of this tension between suffering and victory. It says that the Servant's exaltation would be preceded by an experience so terrible that he would be disfigured beyond recognition (Isa 52:13–15). And then it goes on to introduce the Servant as a "young plant" and a "root" from the stump of Jesse (Isa 53:1–3). These verses tell about the humble origins of the Servant and link him with the promise to David (2 Sam 7:8–16), after whom the messianic dynasty was named.[4]

This Servant would be disfigured, and his disfigurement would be so horrible that those who witnessed his suffering would despise and reject him, and hide their faces from him (Isa 53:3). But, as it turns out, the "infirmities" and "diseases" that would lead people to hide their faces would actually be their own (vv. 4–6). The text says that the iniquities of "us all" are laid on "him" (v. 6).

1. E.g., Isa 9:2–7, 11:1–3, 53:6–7. The interpretation of each of these passages is, of course, intensely disputed. For the debates, see the standard commentaries on Isaiah.

2. Sawyer, *Fifth Gospel*.

3. These passages include: Isa 42:1–6, 49:1–6, 50:4–9, 52:13—53:12. In medieval times, Rashi popularized the view that the prophet is talking about the nation of Israel. The messianic interpretation of the Servant Songs, however, has a long history of interpretation, going all the way back to at least the first century AD, if not before (Hawkins, "Concept of Suffering Messiah," 12–13).

4. Jeremiah prophecies the restoration of the Davidic dynasty. However, neither 1 Sam 7:8–16 nor Jer 33:14–22 uses the title "messiah." The first actual occurrence of the term is in Dan 9:25, where it is used for a future leader. The expectation of both prophets, however, seems to be for the fulfillment of the promises made to David, and one may therefore infer that the descendant of David promised in 1 Sam 7:8–16 will be the messiah.

He is described as one "like a lamb that is led to the slaughter" (Isa 53:7) and whose life would be made into an "offering" (*asham*) (v. 10). This is a reference to the guilt offering, which was one of the sacrifices that the Israelites made to atone for sin.[5] Just as the life of the sacrificial animal was brought to an end in the process of being offered up, so too the Servant would be "cut off" (Isa 53:8), "crushed" (v. 10), "poured out . . . to death" (v. 12), and put in a grave (v. 9). The prophet explains that, by serving as a guilt offering, the Servant "shall make many righteous" and "shall bear their iniquities" (vv. 11–12). The prophet Isaiah clearly understands the death of the Servant as being substitutionary. The Servant would suffer and die on behalf of God's people.

Like a lamb to the slaughter

The gospel writers interpret much of Jesus's ministry on the basis of Isaiah's Servant.[6] Matthew draws on Isa 42 and 43 as the

---

5. Cf. Lev 5:14—6:7, 7:1–6.

6. Among the many classic studies on the New Testament's interpretation and appropriation of Isa 53, see France, "Servant of the Lord"; Hooker, *Jesus the Servant*; Lindsey, *Servant Songs*; North, *Suffering Servant in Deutero-Isaiah*; Wolf, *Interpreting Isaiah*; Zimmerli and Jeremias, *Servant of God*. For more recent study and bibliography, see Bock and Glaser, *Gospel According to Isaiah 53*.

background for Jesus's healing ministry.[7] And Luke uses Isa 53 to explain why Jesus was numbered with the transgressors.[8]

But, most importantly for us, New Testament writers draw on Isa 53 to interpret Jesus's death on the cross. In Acts 8, the Holy Spirit sends Philip to an Ethiopian eunuch who is riding in a chariot and reading the book of Isaiah. Philip asks the man if he understands what he was reading, and he says, "How can I, unless someone guides me?" (Acts 8:31). The passage he is reading is Isa 53:6–7, which reads: "He was led like a sheep to the slaughter, and as a lamb before its shearer is silent, so he did not open his mouth. In his humiliation he was deprived of justice. Who can speak of his descendants? For his life was taken from the earth" (NIV). The eunuch asks Philip to explain to him what the passage means, and Philip uses that passage to preach the good news about Jesus (Acts 8:34–35).

Later on, the apostle Peter draws on Isa 53 to interpret the death of Jesus. He writes, "He himself bore our sins in his body on the cross, so that, having died to sins, we might live for righteousness; by his wounds you have been healed. For you were going astray like sheep, but now you have returned to the shepherd and guardian of your souls" (1 Pet 2:24–25).

Daniel's Anointed One Who Would Be "Cut Off"

Daniel was one of many Judeans who was carried off into exile in Babylon in the days of Nebuchadnezzar (in 605 BC), where he lived in exile his entire life. In Dan 9, the prophet ponders a prophecy from Jeremiah that deals with the LORD's promise to deliver his people from their exile (Jer 29:10–14). As he ponders this passage, he breaks into a prayer of repentance on behalf of himself and the entire community of Judean exiles (Dan 9:1–19).

---

7. With regard to healing the sick, Matt 8:17 alludes to Isa 53:4, and Matt 12:18–21 cites almost all of Isa 42:1–4.

8. In Luke 22:37, he cites Isa 53:12, "And he was numbered with the transgressors."

While he is praying, the angel Gabriel appears to him to give him insight into the prophecy of Jeremiah. The angel explains that a definite period of time (seventy weeks) has been decreed by God for the accomplishment of the restoration of his people from bondage. Daniel 9:25 identifies the beginning of the period and the length of time until the appearance of a "messianic prince" (my translation). The period would begin with "the time that the word went out to restore and rebuild Jerusalem," which is probably a reference to the proclamation of Cyrus that allowed the Jews to return to their homeland (ca. 538 BC). The time from the beginning point of the prophecy until the appearance of the messianic prince is said to be "seven sevens and sixty-two sevens." The seven sevens probably symbolize the period between the first return from exile and the completion of the work of Ezra and Nehemiah, and the sixty-two sevens may symbolize the period between that time and the first coming of Jesus.[9]

In any case, our interest here is on what would happen to the Messiah after this period of time. Daniel says that, after the completion of the sixty-two sevens, the Messiah would be "cut off" and would "have nothing" or "no one" (Dan 9:26). He clearly intends to say that the Messiah would be killed, but his choice of words is interesting. Instead of using the regular word "kill" (*harag*), he uses the verb "cut" (*karath*). This word can be used for cutting things down, like trees, for example (e.g., Deut 19:5). It is also used for beheading (1 Sam 5:4) and, in that case, certainly means "kill." One of the most important uses of this word is in covenant-making contexts. While English translations of the Old Testament always say that someone "made" a covenant, the Hebrew actually says that they "cut" (*karath*) a covenant (e.g., Gen 15:18). This refers to the fact that, in order to ratify a covenant in Old Testament times, an animal would be slaughtered.[10] Could it

---

9. The interpretation of this material is intensely disputed, with approaches ranging from preterist, historicist, and premillennial. A thorough discussion of the range of interpretive possibilities goes way beyond our purposes here. Suffice it to say, my approach here is essentially preterist. For this approach in Daniel, see Mangano, *Esther & Daniel*; Steinmann, *Daniel*; Young, *Daniel*.

10. Elmer Smick, "כָּרַת (*karat*)," *TWOT* 1:456–57.

be that the author of Daniel chose the word "cut" rather than "kill" because of its covenant associations? Was he trying to say that the death of the Messiah had covenantal connotations?

Jesus certainly applied Daniel's statement that the Messiah would "have nothing" (Dan 9:26 NIV) or "no one" to himself. Before his arrest, Jesus tells the disciples that they will scatter and abandon him (John 16:32). The Gospel of Matthew relates how Jesus's robe is taken from him and how, when he has been crucified, his clothes are divided up by the casting of lots (Matt 27:31, 35). And, as he hangs on the cross, he feels that even God has turned his back on him (Matt 27:46). The apostle Paul tells the Corinthian church that Jesus, although he was rich, became poor for their sake (2 Cor 8:9). While none of these passages contains a clear linguistic connection to Dan 9:26, they all echo the basic idea of that text: when the Messiah is "cut off," everything he has is taken away and he is abandoned by everyone.

Zechariah's Pierced Messiah

After the exile, Zechariah prophesies to those Jews who have re-turned to Jerusalem from Babylon.[11] He urges them to rebuild the temple that has been destroyed more than sixty-five years be-fore in 586 BC, when the Babylonians invaded Jerusalem (Zech 4:9–10; 6:12). In Zech 11, the prophet takes up the image of the shepherd, which was a common metaphor for both leaders and deities in the ancient world.[12] The Lord is often called Israel's shepherd,[13] but when the term is applied to political leaders in the Old Testament, it is used only in negative ways.

For example, in Ezekiel, the prophet pronounces a series of woe oracles against Judah's derelict "shepherds" (34:1–10). Ezekiel prophesies that the Lord will rescue his people from these bad

---

11. Zechariah began his prophetic career in the second year of Darius, king of Persia (520 BC), about sixteen years after the first company of Judeans returned from the Babylonian exile.

12. Gerald L. Mattingly, "Shepherd," *HBD* 951–52.

13. E.g., Ps 23:1, Isa 40:11, Mic 7:14, Ps 80:1.

shepherds, and he will do it by raising up a good shepherd and establishing a "covenant of peace" (34:23–31). Ezekiel does not call this good shepherd the Messiah, but he does say that he will be "my servant David" (34:23), which clearly links this prophecy to the promise to David (2 Sam 7:8–16).

Zechariah's use of the shepherd imagery is in the context of a discussion about Judah's leadership. He contrasts two kinds of shepherds, one of whom will abuse the flock (Zech 11:4–17) and the other of whom will suffer for the flock (13:7–9). In the latter passage, the shepherd is an associate of the LORD, upon whom he calls his sword to strike, so "that the sheep may be scattered" (13:7). The identity of this stricken shepherd is debated. Some have identified him as a Davidic ruler.[14] Others identify him as the high priest who represented the Jewish community before the Persian king.[15]

However, based on the way that Zechariah uses the theme of good and bad shepherds, it would seem most reasonable to conclude that he is referring to the true messianic shepherd. And he is saying that it will be because of the rejection of the messianic shepherd that God's people will be scattered. The scattering of the Hebrew people was one of the curses for covenant disobedience (Deut 28:64), and when the shepherd is struck, the sheep will be scattered in fulfillment of that curse.[16]

In Zech 12, the prophet looks forward to a time when God's people will experience complete deliverance from sin. In that day, he says that the LORD will pour out upon the house of David a spirit of compassion, and that "when they look on the one whom they have pierced, they shall mourn for him" (Zech 12:10). The traditional Hebrew text of the Old Testament actually has the preposition "to" plus the first common singular pronominal suffix "me," so that the text actually reads that "they will look upon *me* whom they have pierced."[17] This reading seems to say that it is the LORD himself

---

14. E.g., Meyers, "Zechariah," 1349.

15. Ploger, *Theocracy and Eschatology*, 88.

16. E.g., Barker, "Zechariah," 821.

17. Emphasis added. I am referring here to the Masoretic Text, which dates to the medieval period.

who is pierced. Others think that the pierced one is the same as the suffering Servant of Isa 53.[18] According to second-century rabbinic traditions, the pierced one of Zechariah is the Messiah, who is pierced on behalf of God's people.[19]

Conclusions: Rescuing Others by Self-Sacrifice

The idea that someone could rescue others through their own death might seem strange. And yet, there are many examples of this from various realms throughout known history. Warfare provides examples of such sacrifice. In the ancient world, Leonidas intentionally sacrificed himself so that Greece would have time to prepare for the Persian invasion. The sciences also provide many examples. In the twentieth century, for example, the French physicist and chemist Marie Curie (1867–1934) sacrificed herself in the process of developing the theory of radioactivity, inventing techniques for isolating radioactive isotopes, and discovering two elements, polonium and radium. Her repeated exposure to radiation in the course of her scientific research over many years led to her death of aplastic anemia in 1934. There are many examples of men and women who gave their lives so that others might live.

In the Old Testament, the Hebrew prophets anticipated that, eventually, death itself would be defeated when a righteous sufferer would give himself on behalf of humankind. In Jesus Christ, the hope of the ages has been fulfilled. He himself bore our sins in his body on the cross. By his wounds we have been healed. Because he died, we can die to sin and be raised to righteousness.

18. E.g., Merrill, *Haggai, Zechariah, Malachi*, 319–22.

19. According to the Babylonian Talmud (Sukkah 52a), Rabbi Dosa (second century AD) identified the pierced one as Messiah ben Joseph, who would fall in battle in the war against Gog and Magog. This view was also adopted by the famous medieval rabbi Rashi (AD 1040–1105).

Discussion Questions

1. What are the Servant Songs in Isaiah? What do they describe?

2. How did New Testament writers interpret and apply Isaiah's Servant Songs?

3. What does Daniel say would happen to the messianic prince when it came time to restore God's people from bondage?

4. How did Jesus interpret and apply Dan 9:26?

5. What happens to Zechariah's messianic shepherd?

6. Discuss some other examples of people rescuing others through their own deaths.

Chapter 7

Passion/Palm Sunday

By His Death He Broke the Power
of Death (Heb 2:10–18)

IN PREVIOUS CHAPTERS, WE have considered how death came
into the world at the fall, how God deals with it throughout the
Old Testament, and how he will eventually defeat it through
Jesus Christ. What we have seen is that there's a great irony in
Scripture: death is defeated by death. In the book of Exodus, God
commands a Passover lamb to be sacrificed in order to rescue the
Israelites from the angel of death and free them from slavery in
Egypt. At Mt. Sinai, he institutes a sacrificial system that calls for
the regular sacrifice of cattle in order to atone for sin. And, once
we get into the prophets, we see that they begin to teach that,
eventually, the LORD would send a man, a Servant, his Son, to die
on behalf of humankind once and for all. We looked at Isaiah's
Suffering Servant, Daniel's Messiah who would be "cut off," and
Zechariah's "pierced" Messiah.

Sometime between about AD 50 to 90, an early Christian
pastor wrote a sermon about how Jesus is the consummation and
fulfillment of all God's previous saving work. It's come into the

New Testament as the Epistle to the Hebrews.[1] This pastor begins his sermon by saying, "Long ago God spoke to our ancestors in many and various ways by the prophets, but in these last days he has spoken to us by a Son" (Heb 1:1–2). And throughout the book of Hebrews the pastor presents Jesus as the fulfillment of all God's saving work, especially the ancient sacrificial services of the tabernacle and the temple. He calls him the "pioneer and perfecter of faith" (12:2). But, in order for Jesus to fulfill the saving work God had been doing throughout Old Testament times, the pastor argues that he first had to become human and become subject to death so that he could defeat it.

The Humanity of Jesus

The church teaches that Jesus is the Second Person of the Trinity, the Son of God, who is beyond space and time, and that, in a supreme act of condescension, he left heaven's glory and became flesh. This has come to be known as the "incarnation," after the Latin translation of John 1:14, which says the Word "became flesh." But doesn't this go against the Old Testament? How can the New Testament idea of Jesus as the visible "Son of God" be harmonized with the Old Testament idea that no one could see God and live (Exod 33:20)?

The Old Testament Trajectory toward Incarnation

The idea that no one could look upon the LORD and live to tell the tale was written deeply into Israelite thinking. There were a number of people who had close encounters with God that included some kind of visible physical manifestation of the divine, including Hagar, Jacob, Moses, Gideon, and Manoah.[2] Each of these men

---

1. For a detailed discussion about the authorship and date of the book, as well as the identification of the book as a "Christian synagogue homily," see Cockerill, *Epistle to the Hebrews*, 2–16.

2. Gen 16:13, 32:30; Exod 33:20–23; Judg 6:22, 13:22.

and women had remarkable experiences of a visible manifestation of God. However, these encounters left them terrified and simply proved the rule that no one expected to see God and live.

And yet, there is a trajectory toward incarnation in the Old Testament. In each of the foregoing examples, men and women encounter a physical representation of God. In the cases of Hagar, Jacob, Gideon, and Manoah, their encounter is with the "angel of the LORD" or even simply "a man." In each case, the one receiving the visit realizes in retrospect that their visitor was actually a manifestation of God himself, and this realization causes fear and trembling.

The case of Moses is a bit different. When he came upon the bush that was burning but not consumed, the text reports that the "angel of the LORD appeared to him in a flame of fire" from within the bush (Exod 3:2). And yet, when Moses drew closer, God said to him, "I am the God of your father, the God of Abraham, the God of Isaac, and the God of Jacob" (v. 4). Once God had said this, "Moses hid his face, for he was afraid to look at God" (v. 6). But, instead of striking Moses dead, God assured him that he would be with him (v. 12). Later, when they had received the Ten Commandments from God at Mt. Sinai, the Israelites said: "Look, the LORD our God has shown us his glory and greatness, and we have heard his voice out of the fire. We have seen this day that God may speak to someone and the person may still live" (Deut 5:24).

In later Israelite history, several of the prophets received partial visions of God's physical form. Isaiah has an impressive vision of the "hem" of the LORD's robe, which fills the temple (Isa 6:1). Ezekiel opens the door a bit further and sees God in a human outline, but with such a dazzling splendor that nothing more can be seen or said (Ezek 1:25–28). The sixth-century prophet Daniel, however, sees God in all his glory and describes in detail the features of the Ancient of Days: "As I watched, thrones were set in place, and an Ancient One took his throne; his clothing was white as snow, and the hair of his head like pure wool; his throne was fiery flames, and its wheels were burning fire. A stream of fire issued and flowed out from his presence. A thousand thousands served him, and ten thousand times ten thousand stood attending him" (Dan 7:9–10).

A bit later in Daniel's vision, the messianic Son of Man comes into presence of the Ancient of Days, and he is described as "one like a son of man, coming with the clouds of heaven" (Dan 7:13 NIV). He is clearly a celestial figure, since he is given power and authority, which evokes the worship of "all peoples, nations, and languages" (7:14)

By the time we get to the intertestamental period, the title "Son of Man" had come to be recognized as the title of a divine Messiah (e.g., 1 En. 46:1–2).[3] It is clear that, by this time, some Jews clearly expected God to come down to earth and take human form.[4]

The Mystery of the Incarnation

Even if a trajectory toward incarnation can be tracked from the Old Testament to the New Testament, this does not eliminate its mystery. The incarnation remains an unfathomable mystery that is enshrined in early Christian hymns. Paul quotes one of the earliest of these hymns in his Letter to the Philippians, when he says that Christ Jesus

> who, though he was in the form of God,
> did not regard equality with God
>   as something to be grasped,
> but emptied himself,
>   taking the form of a slave,
>   assuming human likeness.
> And being found in appearance as a human,
>   he humbled himself. (Phil 2:6–8)

---

3. First Enoch was written ca. second to first century BC.
4. Boyarin, *Jewish Gospels*, 34.

Before the incarnation, Christ had a form and status equal to God,[5] but he "emptied himself" by taking human form.[6] He went even lower than that, in that he took on the status of a slave, the lowest possible human status. This song has come to be known as the kenosis, from the Greek verb *kenoō* (empty) in v. 7, because it recounts Christ's supreme self-renunciation, when he divested himself of his heavenly glory to become a man. This is a bottomless mystery. Why in the world would the Second Person of the Trinity, the Son of God, empty himself in this way to become an ordinary human being, with all the limitations that come with the human condition?

In James Denny's classic study on *The Death of Christ*, first published in 1902, the Scottish Free Church theologian explains that "the view of St. Paul and of primitive Christianity generally, [was] that sin and death were so related to one another—were in some sense, indeed, so completely one—that no one could undertake the responsibility of sin who did not at the same time submit to death."[7]

In other words, if someone is going to overcome sin and death, it has to be someone *subject* to sin and death. It is the same as if someone wanted to win the Heisman Trophy, he would have to become a college football player. Or if someone wanted to win the World Heavyweight Championship, he would have to become a boxer. Or if someone wanted to win the World Artistic Gymnastics Championships, she would have to become a gymnast. This principle illustrates the necessity of the incarnation.

And the author of Hebrews certainly follows this logic. He explains that Jesus was "made lower than the angels for a little while" (Heb 2:9). He came to be "of the same family" with humanity (2:11). And he gets to the heart of the purpose of the incarnation when he says, "Since, therefore, the children share flesh and blood, he himself likewise shared the same things, so that through

5. E.g., John 1:1–18, Col 1:15–20.

6. The hymn the pastor quotes has come to be known as the kenosis, from the Greek verb *kenoō* (empty), which is used in Phil 2:7.

7. Denney, *Death of Christ*, 229.

death he might destroy the one who has the power of death, that is, the devil, and free those who all their lives were held in slavery by the fear of death" (2:14–15).

Breaking the Power of Him Who Holds the Power of Death

According to these verses, there were two reasons for Christ's incarnation: first, that he might break the power of the one who holds the power of death; and second, that he might free those enslaved by their fear of death.

The Devil Holds the Power of Death

The pastor names the devil[8] as the one "who has the power of death" (v. 14). This is somewhat of a puzzling statement, since we might have expected him to say that God has the power of death, since he's the Creator and God of all. And yet, there are numerous statements in the New Testament about the authority of the devil. For example, in the Gospel of John, the apostle calls Satan "the ruler of this world" (John 12:31; 14:30). In his first epistle, he says that "the whole world lies under the power of the evil one" (1 John 5:19). The apostle Paul identifies Satan as "the god of this world" (2 Cor 4:4) and the "prince of the power of the air, the spirit that is now at work in the sons of disobedience" (Eph 2:2 ESV).

William Lane is probably right when he explains, "The devil did not possess control over death inherently but gained his power when he seduced humankind to rebel against God" (Gen 3).[9] As the seventeenth-century churchman John Owen says in his classic commentary on Hebrews, "All of Satan's power over death was founded on sin. The obligation of the sinner to death gave

---

8. The term "devil" (διάβολος) was the Greek translation of the Hebrew term "Satan" (שׂטן), which means "accuser" or "slanderer." He appears in the Old Testament (Job 2:1–4, 6–7; Zech 3:1–2; 1 Chr 21:1) and in later Jewish writings (Wis 2:24, 18:15; T.Ab. 13:1) as the personification of evil.

9. Lane, *Hebrews 1–8*, 61.

Satan his power. If this obligation was removed, Satan's power would also be taken away."[10]

By His Death Jesus Broke the Power of Death

The author of Hebrews says that Jesus became human so that "through death he might destroy the one who has the power of death, that is, the devil" (Heb 2:14). If the power of death was the result of human sin, then it was Jesus's death that broke that power by atoning for sin. His death was an atoning death. And this is a theme the pastor repeats throughout his sermon.

- He explains that Jesus was a merciful and faithful high priest in that he made atonement for the sins of the people (2:17).

- He says that Christ appeared once for all "to do away with sin by the sacrifice of himself" (9:26 NIV).

- He talks about Christ being offered to bear the sins of many (9:28).

- He proclaims that Jesus offered one sacrifice for sins forever and perfected forever by that sacrifice those who are being sanctified (10:12–14).

The pastor also talks about the blood of Christ with the same sacrificial conception. He says:

- The blood of Christ will purge your conscience from acts that lead to death (9:14).

- We have boldness to enter into the most holy place through the blood of Jesus (10:19).

- His blood is the blood of the covenant with which we are sanctified (10:29).

In all these ways the death of Christ is defined as a sacrificial death that broke the power of death by atoning for sin.

10. Owen, *Hebrews*, 46.

Christ crucified

And He Freed Those Held in Slavery by Their Fear of Death

The second thing Jesus accomplished by his death was that he freed those held in slavery by their fear of death (Heb 2:15). Earlier, in chapter 2, we talked about the fear, anger, and hostility with which death was viewed in the Old Testament. One of the reasons for the terror of death was the judgment incurred by sin. The pastor says in Heb 9:27 that "it is appointed for mortals to die once and after that the judgment." A little later he says that it is a "fearful thing to fall into the hands of the living God" (10:31), who is a "consuming fire" (12:29). And so Jesus frees people from the "fear of death" through his sacrificial death, which removes the sin that brings judgment (Heb 2:16–18).[11]

This does not mean that Jesus has annihilated or obliterated the devil and death.[12] Their destruction is not yet complete, and the

---

11. Cockerill, *Epistle to the Hebrews*, 146.

12. The verb used in v. 14 is *katargeō*, which the NRSV translates as "destroy." The NIV translates it as having to do with breaking the power of the devil rather than destroying him completely, and this is probably more accurate here, since the pastor presumes the continued existence of death and evil.

final overthrow of the devil and death will occur only at the end of time.[13] But because of his atoning death, he has removed the terrors of death. Peter O'Brien explains, "Since death cannot separate Christ's people from God's love (Rom 8:38–39), it can no longer be held over our heads by the devil as a means of intimidation."[14]

Conclusions

In these verses from the Epistle to the Hebrews, the pastor has brought together the themes of substitutionary atonement and Christus Victor, or Christ as victor.[15] He interprets Jesus's death through the lens of the Old Testament sacrificial system. He proclaims that Jesus's death provided atonement for the sins of the people. And he also preaches that Jesus's death broke the power of the devil and frees us from the fear of death. Through Jesus's atoning death, he removes the sin that brings the judgment associated with death. In Rom 8, Paul asks,

> What, then, are we to say about these things? If God is for us, who is against us? He who did not withhold his own Son but gave him up for us all, how will he not with him also give us everything else? Who will bring any charge against God's elect? It is God who justifies. Who is to condemn? It is Christ who died, or rather, who was raised, who is also at the right hand of God, who also intercedes for us. Who will separate us from the love of Christ? Will affliction or distress or persecution or famine or nakedness or peril or sword? (Rom 8:31–35).

And he goes on to answer: "No, in all these things we are more than victorious through him who loved us. For I am convinced that neither death, nor life, nor angels, nor rulers, nor things present,

---

13. Cf. Rev 12:7–8, 20:1–3, 10; 1 Cor 5:5, 15:24–26; 2 Tim 1:10.

14. O'Brien, *Letter to the Hebrews*, 116.

15. Schreiner, *Commentary on Hebrews*, 105. Christus Victor, which means "Christ the Victor," is a classical theological paradigm that understands the atonement primarily as a triumph over Satan. For a classic presentation of this view, see Aulén, *Christus Victor*.

nor things to come, nor powers, nor height, nor depth, nor anything else in all creation will be able to separate us from the love of God in Christ Jesus our Lord" (Rom 8:37–39).

This is the victory we share in Christ Jesus!

Discussion Questions

1. What does the author of Hebrews teach is necessary to fulfill the saving work God had been doing throughout Old Testament times?

2. Is the idea of the incarnation contrary to the Old Testament's teaching that no one could look upon God and live? Why or why not?

3. For the author of the Letter to the Hebrews, why was the incarnation necessary?

4. How does the author of Hebrews understand Jesus's death? What did it accomplish?

5. What does the term Christus Victor mean? What does Christ's victory mean to you?

Chapter 8

The Last Enemy
to Be Destroyed

(1 Cor 15:20–28)

THE PASTOR WHO WROTE the Epistle to the Hebrews says that
people live their lives in fear of death (Heb 2:15). We sometimes
think of death, but we try to put it out of our minds. When we
are faced with it, it is a jarring reality. I am reminded of the story
of a man who went to the doctor for some tests, and when it
came time for the doctor to give the test results to the patient, the
doctor said, "Sir, I have some *bad* news for you and some *really
bad* news for you."

The patient was startled, but he managed to regain his com-
posure, and he asked, "Okay, what's the bad news?"

The doctor replied, "The bad news is that you only have
twenty-four hours to live."

The patient was shaken to the core. He swallowed, caught his
breath, and asked, "Well, it can't get any worse than that, can it?
What's the really bad news?"

THE LAST ENEMY TO BE DESTROYED

The doctor replied sheepishly, "Well, the really bad news is that my nurse gave me your test results yesterday and told me to call you pronto."[1]

Needless to say, this patient was deeply distressed!

In the previous chapter, we talked about how, by his death on the cross, Jesus broke the power of sin and death and freed those held in slavery all their lives by their fear of death (Heb 2:14–15). And yet, how can death be said to have been defeated as long as people remain in their graves? In this chapter, we will explore several ideas that began to develop late in the Old Testament period and burgeoned during the intertestamental and New Testament periods. These are the beliefs in a general resurrection, with punishments for the wicked and rewards for the righteous.

The General Resurrection

Late in the Old Testament period, the idea of a general resurrection, when all people would be raised from the dead, began to appear. The idea is first expressed in the years leading up to the exile, after Israel had lived in defiance of the stipulations of the covenant for many years, and as a consequence, God had withdrawn the covenant blessings and instead imposed the covenantal curses (cf. Deut 28). Those who had remained faithful to the LORD suffered unjustly during these times, and despaired over the injustice of their experiences. They lived lives of faithfulness to the LORD, and yet they were punished along with the unrighteous. Would they ever receive the promised covenantal blessings?

Some of the later prophets began to proclaim that, in the latter days, the LORD would vindicate his people. For those who had already died, this implied that they would be raised in order to receive their reward. The idea begins to appear in Isaiah, Ezekiel, and Daniel, but it is sketchy. It is not until we get into the New Testament that the idea is developed more fully.

---

1. Evans, *Book of Illustrations*, 189–90.

A General Resurrection in the Old Testament

The idea of a general resurrection appears in two passages in Isa 24–27, a section of the book that is often referred to as "the Isaiah apocalypse."[2] In the first passage, Isaiah prophecies that a time will come when the LORD will vindicate Israel, with implications for the entire world. At that time, the LORD will prepare a sumptuous feast on Mt. Zion "for all peoples" (Isa 25:6). This extravagant feast will be accompanied by the LORD putting an end to death and mourning. Isaiah proclaims: "On this mountain he will destroy the shroud that enfolds all peoples, the sheet that covers all nations; he will swallow up death forever. The Sovereign LORD will wipe away the tears from all faces; he will remove his people's disgrace from all the earth" (Isa 25:7–8 NIV).

Among some of ancient Israel's neighbors, death was a god named "Mot"[3] who had a voracious appetite and was constantly swallowing people up.[4] And, while the Israelites were forbidden from worshiping the pagan gods, there is evidence in the Scriptures that they at times personified death as well (e.g., Ps 49:14). But Isaiah says that the LORD will eventually turn the tables on death. Instead of death swallowing people up, the LORD "will swallow up death forever" (Isa 25:8).

The second Isaianic passage follows a lament, in which God's people despair over the effects of death. They lament, "The dead do not live; shades do not rise because you have punished and destroyed them and wiped out all memory of them" (Isa 26:14). Even having babies is futile because, when a woman gives birth, she may as well be giving birth to wind, since her children will ultimately die too (v. 19). But Isaiah prophesies that the LORD will eventually reverse these depressing conditions. He promises, "Your dead shall live, their corpses shall rise. Those who dwell in the dust will awake

---

2. For a succinct discussion, see Coggins, "Isaiah," 454–55.

3. From the Hebrew *maveth* (מָוֶת).

4. For references to the insatiable appetite of Mot, see examples in the Ugaritic Baal Cycle in Coogan and Smith, *Stories from Ancient Canaan*, 96–153.

and shout for joy! For your dew is a radiant dew, and the earth will give birth to those long dead" (Isa 26:19).

In the sixth century BC, Ezekiel, who had been among the first group of Jerusalemites to be carried away to Babylon in the exile,[5] had a vision that was originally about the restoration of exile but came to be understood as anticipating the general resurrection. The vision depicted a battlefield on which thousands of corpses lay, who collectively represented dead Israel after the Babylonian invasion (Ezek 37:1–2). Having been exiled from the promised land, it was as if they were dead. The LORD asked Ezekiel whether the dry bones could live again. His question was not about whether dead individuals could live again, but about whether Israel could ever be restored. Ezekiel answered that only the LORD knew (v. 3). The LORD commanded Ezekiel to issue various prophecies, and through the course of the prophet's pronouncements, the corpses were reanimated, "and they lived and stood on their feet, a vast multitude" (v. 10). While this prophecy clearly had to do with the possibility of return from exile, both Jews and Christians later interpreted it as a prophesy of the resurrection of the dead at the end of time.[6]

The final Old Testament passage that speaks about a general resurrection is in Daniel. The prophet Daniel, who wrote in the context of the Babylonian exile, proclaims that, at the end of days, "multitudes who sleep in the dust of the earth will awake: some to everlasting life, others to shame and everlasting contempt" (Dan 12:2 NIV). This is the only passage in the Old Testament that states that there will be different destinies for the righteous and the wicked.[7]

5. This would have been about 598 BC. Cf. the account in 2 Kgs 24:10–17.

6. Cf. Block, *Book of Ezekiel*, 388–92.

7. These ideas were developed further in the period between the Old and New Testaments. See esp. Wis 2:12–20, 3:1–9; 2 Macc 7:1–42.

The general resurrection

A General Resurrection in the New Testament

In the New Testament, the idea of a general resurrection is developed more fully. In the Gospel of John, when the Jewish leaders begin to oppose him, Jesus defends himself and says: "Do not be astonished at this, for the hour is coming when all who are in their graves will hear his voice and will come out: those who have done good to the resurrection of life, and those who have done evil to the resurrection of condemnation" (John 5:28–29).

In the parable of the sheep and the goats, Jesus teaches, "When the Son of Man comes in his glory and all the angels with him, then he will sit on the throne of his glory. All the nations will be gathered before him, and he will separate people one from another as a shepherd separates the sheep from the goats" (Matt 25:31–32).

At the end of the parable, the Son of Man condemns some to eternal punishment but rewards the righteous with eternal life (v. 46).

The apostle Paul, in his speech before Felix, talks about the general resurrection. He says: "But this I admit to you, that according to the Way, which they call a sect, I worship the God of our ancestors, believing everything laid down according to the law or written in the prophets. I have a hope in God—a hope that they themselves also accept—that there will be a resurrection of both the righteous and the unrighteous. Therefore I do my best always to have a clear conscience toward God and all people" (Acts 24:14–15). Paul believed there would be a general resurrection, and this was the majority view of Jews in Judea and Galilee.

At the end of the New Testament, the apostle John recorded a vision of the general resurrection. He wrote: "And I saw the dead, great and small, standing before the throne, and books were opened. Also another book was opened, the book of life. And the dead were judged according to their works, as recorded in the books. And the sea gave up the dead that were in it, Death and Hades gave up the dead that were in them, and all were judged according to what they had done" (Rev 20:12–13).

In John's vision, he makes it clear that no one will be left out of this resurrection. Those who have not been buried, but whose bodies have been lost at sea, will be raised. And even those who have already gone to Hades, the realm of the dead, will be raised for judgment.

Paul's Discussion of the General Resurrection in 1 Corinthians 15

The most comprehensive teaching on resurrection in the New Testament is in 1 Cor 15, in which the apostle Paul discusses Jesus's resurrection and the general resurrection of the dead. He starts out by reminding the Corinthians of his earlier preaching among them (vv. 1–2). The resurrection of Jesus Christ has been a foundational part of his proclamation. He says:

> For I handed on to you as of first importance what I in
> turn had received: that Christ died for our sins in accor-
> dance with the scriptures, and that he was buried, and
> that he was raised on the third day in accordance with
> the scriptures, and that he appeared to Cephas, then to
> the twelve. Then he appeared to more than five hundred
> brothers and sisters at one time, most of whom are still
> alive, though some have died. Then he appeared to James,
> then to all the apostles. Last of all, as to one untimely
> born, he appeared also to me. (1 Cor 15:3–8 NIV)

In these verses, Paul quotes an early Christian formula that reflects the earliest proclamation of the church: Christ died, was
buried, and was raised on the third day.[8] Scholars agree that the
quote begins in v. 3, but they disagree about the extent of the
quoted text.[9] It seems to run from vv. 3 to 5, after which Paul
gives his own impressive list of witnesses to the resurrection of
Jesus (vv. 6–8). From this and other creedal formulas, hymn frag-
ments, and other traditions embedded in Paul's epistles, it is clear
that the resurrection of Christ was the foundation of every aspect
of the early church's faith.[10]

---

8. Early Christian formulations were identified and discussed by form crit-
ics like C. H. Dodd, *Apostolic Preaching*; and Reginald Fuller, *Foundations*. For
recent discussion, see Nickelsburg, "Resurrection," 5:688.

9. For a detailed discussion, see Conzelmann, *1 Corinthians*, 251–57.

10. Fuller, *Christ and Christianity*, 74–82.

The resurrection of Jesus Christ

Indeed, the resurrection should be understood as the completion of Jesus's atoning work on the cross. Dietrich Bonhoeffer explains, "The resurrection of Jesus Christ is God's 'yes' to Christ and his atoning work."[11] In Rom 4:25, Paul links the cross and the resurrection together, explaining that "Jesus was handed over to death for our trespasses and raised for our justification." Furthermore, in 1 Cor 15:17, he announces, "If Christ has not been raised, your faith is futile, and you are still in your sins." So, our being made righteous does not depend solely on Jesus's death, but also on his resurrection.

When Paul first proclaimed the resurrection of Christ to the Corinthians, they accepted his message (v. 11), but they had some misunderstandings about what the resurrection meant. And so

11. Bonhoeffer, *I Want to Live*, 116.

Paul goes on to discuss Jesus's resurrection in general, as well as to correct some of their misconceptions. Although they believed that Christ had been raised from the dead, some of them did not believe that there would be a general resurrection (v. 12). It appears that they had come to understand the idea of the resurrection as a sort of spiritualized present life.[12] But Paul insists that this cannot be, and he goes on to argue that the resurrection is critical for Christian faith. He explains,

> If there is no resurrection of the dead, then not even Christ has been raised. And if Christ has not been raised, our preaching is useless and so is your faith. More than that, we are then found to be false witnesses about God, for we have testified about God that he raised Christ from the dead. But he did not raise him if in fact the dead are not raised. For if the dead are not raised, then Christ has not been raised either. And if Christ has not been raised, your faith is futile; you are still in your sins. Then those also who have fallen asleep in Christ are lost. If only for this life we have hope in Christ, we are of all people most to be pitied. (1 Cor 15:13–19 NIV)

Paul connects the resurrection of Jesus with the general resurrection, and he insists that you cannot have one without the other.

He goes on to develop this argument with an analogy from Israelite farming practices. He explains that "Christ has indeed been raised from the dead, the firstfruits of those who have fallen asleep. For since death came through a man, the resurrection of the dead comes also through a man. For as in Adam all die, so in Christ all will be made alive. But each in turn: Christ, the firstfruits; then, when he comes, those who belong to him" (vv. 20–23 NIV).

In the Old Testament, the Israelites were instructed to give the "firstfruits" of their harvests to the LORD as an offering.[13] The "firstfruits" were the first signs of the harvest, and once the harvest had begun, the rest of the harvest was certain.

---

12. See Paul's remarks in 1 Cor 4:8–11.

13. Exod 23:16, 19.

Paul uses the analogy of the firstfruits to explain the relationship between the resurrection of Christ and his followers. He says that Jesus is the firstfruits of the resurrection, which means that the resurrection of "those who belong to him" is sure to follow when the harvest is completed (v. 23). It will be completed "when he comes" (v. 23), which is, of course, a reference to the second coming.[14] When Christ returns, he will destroy "all dominion, authority and power," and will reign "until he has put all his enemies under his feet" (v. 25).

Paul concludes his argument by saying that "the last enemy to be destroyed is death" (v. 26). There's a sense in which death *began* to be destroyed when Jesus was raised from the dead. And yet, how can death be said to have been defeated as long as people remain in their graves? Gordon Fee explains, "As long as people die, God's own sovereign purposes are not yet fully realized."[15] This is because death is a result of the fall. And as long as people die, they are still experiencing the consequences of sin.

The Corinthians asked, "How are the dead raised?" and "With what kind of body will they come?" (v. 35 NIV). The Corinthians were incredulous. How can a corpse be reanimated? Contemporary readers may be surprised by Paul's answer to these questions. He replies, "How foolish!" and uses an analogy from nature to answer to their questions. He explains, "What you sow does not come to lie unless it dies" (v. 36). When a person wants to grow a plant, they must first put a seed into the ground, which has to "die" in the earth before it will then sprout. Furthermore, Paul points out that the plant that sprouts forth looks nothing like the seed that was planted. Rather, it looks completely different (v. 37).

Verlyn Verbrugge emphasizes that this is an analogy and that we should be careful about taking it too far.[16] For one thing, we should not try to read Paul's statement through the lens of modern

---

14. The Greek word *parousia* (παρουσια) was used in the political sphere for the arrival of a ruler, and in the religious realm for the appearance of the deity. Paul uses the term also in 1 Thess 2:19, 3:13, 4:15; 5:23; 2 Thess 2:1, 8, 9.

15. Fee, *First Epistle to Corinthians*, 838.

16. See Verbrugge, "1 Corinthians," 11:401.

biological science. A seed does not really "die" when it is planted in the ground, but is simply dormant while it awaits the conditions that cause germination. For another thing, we should not conclude that the resurrection of a human body requires death, since Paul goes on to say that those who are alive at the time of Jesus's return will also receive a resurrection body (vv. 51–52).[17]

With those caveats in mind, however, Paul's analogy of the seed powerfully demonstrates the validity of the idea of resurrection. In answer to the questions of the Corinthians, Paul basically says: "*You* hold the answer in your *own* hands. Simply look at the way God has arranged the natural order of the plant life. In the everyday occurrence of the seed you have the evidence to answer your question . . . .[that] *out of death* a new expression of life springs forth."[18]

Paul's logic here is that the general resurrection is a necessity. If death is really to be destroyed and defeated, then it must be robbed of its store of those who do not belong to it because they belong to Christ! And so the final destruction of death "takes place when Christ's own resurrection as firstfruits culminates in the full harvest of the resurrection of those who are his."[19]

17. Cf. also 1 Thess 4:15.
18. Fee, *First Epistle to Corinthians*, 864; emphasis added.
19. Fee, *First Epistle to Corinthians*, 838.

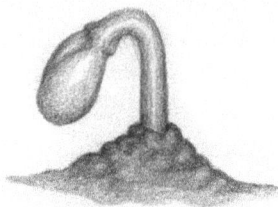

A seed sprouting from the ground

Paul makes this point again at the end of his discussion about the resurrection, where he says that both the living and the dead *must* assume transformed bodies in order for Christ's victory over death to be realized. He explains:

> For this perishable body must put on imperishability, and this mortal body *must* put on immortality. When this perishable body puts on imperishability and this mortal body puts of immortality, then the saying that is written will be fulfilled: "Death has been swallowed up in victory." "Where, O death, is your victory? Where, O death, is your sting?" The sting of death is sin, and the power of sin is the law. But thanks be to God, who gives us the victory through our Lord Jesus Christ." (1 Cor 15:53–56; emphasis added)

If the long chain of death and decay inaugurated by the first Adam has really been defeated in Jesus Christ, then the dead cannot remain in their graves! It is only when the dead are raised up on the last day that death can truly be said to have been defeated![20]

20. Fee, *First Epistle to Corinthians*, 887–88.

To make his point, Paul quotes two Old Testament texts that have not yet been fulfilled. In 1 Cor 15:54, in a modified quote from Isa 25:8, he proclaims that "death has been swallowed up in victory." Once the general resurrection has occurred, death will not be able to tyrannize people anymore, because it will have been "swallowed up" by resurrection.

In 1 Cor 15:55, in light of Jesus's victory over death, Paul taunts death with a modified quote from Hos 13:14b, which reads, "Where, O death, is your victory? Where, O death, is your sting?" It is interesting that, even though his taunt has to do with the *future* resurrection of believers, he expresses it in the *present* tense. "Where, O death, are your plagues? Where, O grave, is your destruction?" People still die in the present, but Paul understands that "the beginning of the End has 'already' set in motion the final victory that for us is still 'not yet.'"[21]

After these two "quotes," Paul goes on to say that not only has *death* been overcome by resurrection, but so have the enemies that have brought death to all—sin and the law. He says that "the sting of death is sin" (v. 56a), and his meaning is obvious. In Pauline theology, sin is the deadly sting that has led to death.[22]

The second line is a bit confusing. Paul says that "the power of sin is the law" (v. 56b), and this is a bit unclear because the law is viewed positively in the Old Testament. Yet, here, he says it is "the power of sin." In order to understand what Paul means here, it is helpful to turn to Romans, in which Paul discusses the relationship between sin and the law at some length. There, he explains that, when there is no law, sin is not charged against anyone's account (Rom 5:13). The law allows us to be able to identify sin. It helps us to know when one's actions are depraved or rebellious. And it enables us to know when someone is in rebellion against God. In these respects, the law leads to condemnation.[23]

At the conclusion of this discussion, Paul erupts in a doxology (1 Cor 15:54–57), in which he gives thanks that Jesus is the

---

21. Fee, *First Epistle to Corinthians*, 890.

22. Cf. Dunn, *Theology of Paul*, 124–26.

23. Cf. also 2 Cor 3:6.

victor over the sin that brought death into the world, and over the law that leads to it.

The End of the Story

Anyone who has ever experienced the loss of a loved one knows what Paul means when he talks about death as an enemy. The realization that our loved one is irretrievably gone sends shock waves of grief. Similarly, those who have received a terrifying medical diagnosis know death as the ultimate threat. And it's for these reasons that Paul's message that death will not have the last word is so profound. God will not allow death to draw the curtains on us or our loved ones. He will not allow death to eclipse who they were and the love that we shared with them.

But we live in a sort of "now-but-not-yet" time. Jesus announced that the kingdom had come near, and we experience many of its benefits already.[24] But, on the other hand, all the promises associated with the coming of the kingdom have not yet been fully realized. The author of Hebrews says, "At present, we do not yet see everything in subjection to him" (Heb 2:8–9). There is still evil in the world. We still struggle with sin. We are still mortal. Paul says that even "we ourselves, who have the firstfruits of the Spirit, groan inwardly as we wait eagerly for our adoption to sonship, the redemption of our bodies" (Rom 8:23). Until that final adoption takes place, he says that our bodies remain "subject to death" (8:10). Death is indeed "the last enemy" (1 Cor 15:26), and it won't finally be destroyed until the general resurrection.

But, given the fact that *Jesus's* resurrection has already happened, and that on the last day he will raise up all those who have been "asleep," the defeat of the last enemy, death, is a certainty. Our stories won't end with our deaths. And the stories of those we love whom we have lost to death are not over. As William Willimon so eloquently says, "When we worship a victorious and

---

24. E.g., Mark 1:15, Eph 2:6.

risen Savior, we've always got more future than we do past."[25] We can have confidence that "the coming climax of our story will be our resurrection."[26]

Discussion Questions

1. What is the general resurrection? When and how did the idea emerge in ancient Israel?

2. What do Isaiah, Ezekiel, and Daniel have to say about the general resurrection?

3. What is the relationship between the cross and the resurrection?

4. What is the relationship between Jesus's resurrection and the general resurrection? What does it mean that Jesus's resurrection is the "firstfruits of those who have fallen asleep"?

5. How does nature demonstrate the validity of the resurrection?

6. In 1 Cor 15:54–55, discuss Paul's use of Isa 25:8 and Hos 13:14.

7. What does it mean for you that Jesus will ultimately vanquish the last enemy, death?

25. Willimon, "Small Church Ministry."

26. Goldingay, *Biblical Theology*, 549.

Bibliography

Allison, Gregg R. *Historical Theology: An Introduction to Christian Doctrine.* Grand Rapids: Zondervan, 2011.

Aulén, Gustaf. *Christus Victor: An Historical Study of the Three Main Types of the Idea of the Atonement.* Translated by A. G. Hebert. New York: Macmillan, 1969.

Azam, Hina. "Religious Holidays and Observances." *EI* 2:971–76.

Barker, Kenneth L. "Zechariah." *EBC* 8:721–833.

Barr, James. *The Garden of Eden and the Hope of Immortality.* Minneapolis: Fortress, 1992.

Barth, Christoph. *God with Us: A Theological Introduction to the Old Testament.* Edited by Geoffrey W. Bromiley. Grand Rapids: Eerdmans, 1991.

Becker, Ernest. *The Denial of Death.* Florence, MA: Free Press, 1985.

Block, Daniel L. *The Book of Ezekiel: Chapters 25–48.* NICOT. Grand Rapids: Eerdmans, 1998.

Bock, Darrell L., and Mitch Glaser, eds. *The Gospel According to Isaiah 53: Encountering the Suffering Servant in Jewish and Christian Theology.* Grand Rapids: Kregel, 2012.

Boda, Mark J. *A Severe Mercy: Sin and Its Remedy in the Old Testament.* Siphrut 1. Winona Lake, IN: Eisenbrauns, 2009.

Bonhoeffer, Dietrich. *I Want to Live These Days with You: A Year of Daily Devotions.* Translated by O. C. Dean Jr. Louisville: Westminster John Knox, 2007.

Boyarin, Daniel. *The Jewish Gospels: The Story of the Jewish Christ.* New York: New Press, 2012.

Brown, Donald. *Human Universals.* New York: McGraw Hill, 1991.

Brueggemann, Walter. *Reverberations of Faith: A Theological Handbook of Old Testament Themes.* Louisville: Westminster John Knox, 2002.

Buechner, Frederick. *Telling the Truth: The Gospel as Tragedy, Comedy, and Fairy Tale.* New York: HarperSanFrancisco, 1977.

Charles, R. H. *The Book of Jubilees.* Jerusalem: Makor, 1972.

Chittister, Joan. *The Liturgical Year: The Spiraling Adventure of the Spiritual Life.* Nashville Thomas Nelson, 2009.

Cockerill, Gareth Lee. *The Epistle to the Hebrews.* NICNT. Grand Rapids: Eerdmans, 2012.

Coggins, R. "Isaiah." In *The Oxford Bible Commentary,* edited by John Barton and John Muddiman, 433–86. New York: Oxford University Press, 2001.

Conzelmann, Hans. *1 Corinthians: A Commentary on the First Epistle to the Corinthians.* Translated by James W. Leitch. Hermeneia. Philadelphia: Fortress, 1975.

Coogan, Michael D., and Mark S. Smith, eds. *Stories from Ancient Canaan.* 2nd ed. Louisville: Westminster John Knox, 2012.

Currid, John D. *Ancient Egypt and the Old Testament.* Grand Rapids: Baker, 1997.

"Death." Wikipedia, last edited Aug. 20, 2024. https://en.wikipedia.org/wiki/Death.

De La Torree, Miguel A. *Santería: The Beliefs and Rituals of a Growing Religion in America.* Grand Rapids: Eerdmans, 2004.

Denney, James. *The Death of Christ.* Repr., New Canaan, CT: Keats, 1981.

Dodd, C. H. *The Apostolic Preaching and Its Developments.* London: Hodder & Stoughton, 1936.

Dunn, James D. G. *The Theology of Paul the Apostle.* Grand Rapids: Eerdmans, 1998.

Durham, John I. *Exodus.* WBC 3. Waco: Word, 1987.

Eusebius. *Preparation for the Gospel.* Translated by Edwin Hamilton Gifford. 2 vols. Eugene, OR: Wipf and Stock, 2002.

Evans, Tony. *Tony Evans' Book of Illustrations: Stories, Quotes, and Anecdotes.* Chicago: Moody, 2009.

Evans-Pritchard, E. E. *Nuer Religion.* Oxford: Clarendon, 1956.

Fee, Gordon D. *The First Epistle to the Corinthians.* Rev. ed. NICNT. Grand Rapids: Eerdmans, 2014.

Fox, Matthew. *Original Blessing: A Primer in Creation Spirituality Presented in Four Paths, Twenty-Six Themes, and Two Questions.* New York: TarcherPerigee, 2000.

France, R. T. "The Servant of the LORD in the Teaching of Jesus." *TynBul* 19 (1968) 26–52.

Fuller, Reginald H. *Christ and Christianity: Studies in the Formation of Christology.* Valley Forge, PA: Trinity, 1994.

———. *The Foundations of New Testament Christology.* New York: Scribner's Sons, 1965.

Goldingay, John. *Biblical Theology: The God of the Christian Scriptures.* Downers Grove, IL: InterVarsity, 2016.

———. *An Introduction to the Old Testament: Exploring Text, Approaches & Issues.* Downers Grove, IL: InterVarsity, 2015.

———. *Old Testament Theology: Israel's Gospel.* Downers Grove, IL: IVP Academic, 2015.

Goodspeed, George S. "Atonement in Non-Christian Religions. IV. Atonement by Substitution." *Biblical World* 17 (1901) 297–306.

Gray, G. B. *Sacrifice in the Old Testament.* New York: KTAV, 1971.

Green, Joel B. "Atonement." *NIDB* 1:345–48.

Guthrie, Donald. *New Testament Theology.* Leicester, UK: Inter-Varsity, 1981.

Hawkins, Ralph K. *Ancient Wisdom for the Good Life.* Peabody, MA: Hendrickson, 2023.

———. "The Concept of a Suffering Messiah: Christian Invention or Jewish Conception?" *NEASB* 57 (2012) 11–24.

———. *Discovering Exodus: Content, Interpretation, Reception.* DBT. Grand Rapids: Eerdmans, 2021.

Hebblethwaite, Benjamin, and Michel Weber. "Arabian Religion, Islam, and Haitian Vodou: The 'Recent African Single-Origin Hypothesis' and the Comparison of World Religions." In *Vodou in the Haitian Experience: A Black Atlantic Perspective,* edited by Celucien L. Joseph and Nixon S. Cleophat, 209–37. Lanham, MD: Lexington, 2016.

Hill, Andrew E., and John H. Walton. *A Survey of the Old Testament.* 4th ed. Grand Rapids: Zondervan, 2024.

Hodge, Charles. *Systematic Theology.* 3 vols. Repr., Peabody, MA: Hendrickson Academic, 1999.

Hooker, Morna D. *Jesus the Servant: The Influence of the Servant Concept of Deutero-Isaiah in the New Testament.* London: SPCK, 1959.

Kik, J. Marcellus. *An Eschatology of Victory.* Phillipsburg, NJ: P&R, 1992.

Lane, William L. *Hebrews 1–8.* WBC 47A. Dallas: Word, 1991.

Levinson, David. "Sacrifice and Offerings." In *Encyclopedia of Religious Rites, Rituals and Festivals,* edited by Frank A. Salmone, 379–80. Religion and Society Encyclopedia. London: Routledge, 2004.

Lewis, C. S. *Family Letters 1905–1931.* Edited by Walter Hooper. Vol. 1 of *Collected Letters.* London: HarperCollins, 2000.

———. *God in the Dock: Essays on Theology and Ethics.* Edited by Walter Hooper. Grand Rapids: Eerdmans, 1970.

Lichtheim, Miriam. "Hymn to the Nile." *AEL* 1:204–10.

Lindow, John. *Handbook of Norse Mythology.* Santa Barbara, CA: ABC-CLIO, 2001.

Lindsey, F. Duane. *The Servant Songs: A Study in Isaiah.* Chicago: Moody, 1985.

Long, Thomas G. *Accompany Them with Singing: The Christian Funeral.* Louisville: Westminster John Knox, 2009.

Mangano, Mark. *Esther & Daniel.* CPNIVC. Joplin, MO: College Press, 2001.

Mattingly, Gerald L. "Shepherd." In *The HarperCollins Bible Dictionary*, edited by Mark A. Powell, 951–52. Rev. ed. New York: HarperOne, 2011.

Mercer, Samuel A. B., trans. *The Pyramid Texts*. 4 vols. New York: Longmans, Green, 1952.

Merrill, Eugene H. *Haggai, Zechariah, Malachi: An Exegetical Commentary*. Chicago: Moody, 1994.

Meyer, Nicholas, dir. *Star Trek II: The Wrath of Khan*. 1982; Hollywood, CA: Paramount, 2013. DVD.

Meyers, Eric. "Zechariah." In *The New Interpreter's Study Bible*, edited by Walter Harrelson, 1337–50. Nashville: Abingdon, 2003.

Mitford, Jessica. *The American Way of Death*. Camp Hill, PA: Simon and Schuster, 1963.

———. *The American Way of Death Revisited*. Repr., New York: Vintage, 2000.

Moyer, James C. "Shades." *NIDB* 5:207–8.

Murrell, Nathaniel Samuel. *Afro-Caribbean Religions: An Introduction to Their Historical, Cultural, and Sacred Traditions*. Philadelphia: Temple University Press, 2009.

Neyrey, Jerome H. "Group Orientation." In *Biblical Social Values and Their Meaning: A Handbook*, edited by John Pilch and Bruce J. Malina, 88–91. Peabody, MA: Hendrickson, 1993.

Nickelsburg, George W. E. "Resurrection (Early Judaism and Christianity)." *ABD* 5:684–91.

North, Christopher R. *The Suffering Servant in Deutero-Isaiah: An Historical and Critical Study*. London: Oxford University Press, 1948.

O'Brien, Peter T. *The Letter to the Hebrews*. Grand Rapids: Eerdmans, 2010.

O'Day, Gail R. "The Gospel According to John." *NIB* 9:491–865.

Orr, James. *The Problem of the Old Testament*. London: Nisbet & Co., 1908.

Owen, John. *Hebrews*. CCC. Wheaton, IL: Crossway, 1998.

Packer, J. I. "Understanding the Bible: Evangelical Hermeneutics." In *Restoring the Vision: Anglican Evangelicals Speak Out*, edited by Melvin Tinker, 39–58. Eastbourne, UK: Monarch, 1990.

Ploger, Otto. *Theocracy and Eschatology*. Translated by S. Rudman. Richmond: John Knox, 1968.

Propp, William H. C. *Exodus 1–18: A New Translation with Introduction and Commentary*. New York: Doubleday, 1999.

Raimi, Sam, dir. *Spider-Man 2*. 2004; Culver City, CA: Sony, 2004. DVD.

Richards, Kent Harold. "Death (Old Testament)." *ABD* 2:108–10.

Ritner, Robert K. "The Great Cairo Hymn of Praise to Amun-Re." *COS* 1:25.

Rutledge, Fleming. *The Undoing of Death: Sermons for Holy Week and Easter*. Grand Rapids: Eerdmans, 2002.

Sailhamer, John H. "Genesis." *EBC* 1:21–331.

Sarna, Nahum M. *Exploring Exodus: The Origins of Biblical Israel*. New York: Schocken, 1996.

Sawyer, J. F. A. *The Fifth Gospel: Isaiah in the History of Christianity*. Cambridge: Cambridge University Press, 1996.

Schreiner, Thomas R. *Commentary on Hebrews*. BTCP. Nashville: B&H, 2015.

Shroyer, Danielle. *Original Blessing: Putting Sin in Its Rightful Place*. Minneapolis: Fortress, 2016.

Sklar, Jay. *Leviticus: An Introduction and Commentary*. TOTC 3. Downers Grove, IL: InterVarsity, 2014.

Steinmann, Andrew E. *Daniel*. ConC. Saint Louis: Concordia, 2008.

Teng, Larry, dir. *Supergirl*. Season 1, episode 20, "Better Angels." Aired Apr. 18, 2016, on CBS.

Tigay, Jeffrey H. "Exodus." In *The Jewish Study Bible*, edited by Adele Berlin and Marc Zvi Brettler, 95–192. 2nd ed. New York: Oxford University Press, 2014

Verbrugge, Verlyn D. "1 Corinthians." *EBC* 11:239–414.

Walton, John H. *Ancient Near Eastern Thought and the Old Testament: Introducing the Conceptual World of the Hebrew Bible*. Grand Rapids: Baker Academic, 2006.

Wessel, Walter, and Mark L. Strauss. "The Gospel of Mark." *EBC* 9:671–989.

Willimon, William. "Small Church Ministry and Discipleship." Lecture given at Watson Memorial United Methodist Church, Chatham, VA, Jan. 22, 2017.

Wolf, Herbert M. *Interpreting Isaiah: The Suffering and Glory of the Messiah*. Grand Rapids: Zondervan, 1985.

Yates, David. *Harry Potter and the Deathly Hallows: Part 2*. 2011; Burbank, CA: Warner, 2016. DVD.

Young, Edward J. *Daniel*. GSC. Grand Rapids: Eerdmans, 1949.

Zimmerli, Walter, and Joachim Jeremias. *The Servant of God*. 2nd ed. London: SCM, 1965.

www.ingramcontent.com/pod-product-compliance
Lightning Source LLC
Chambersburg PA
CBHW020207090426

42734CB00008B/973